LIFE AND DEATH OF THE
AMERICAN
WORKER

THE IMMIGRANTS TAKING ON AMERICA'S LARGEST MEATPACKING COMPANY

———

ALICE DRIVER

ONE SIGNAL
PUBLISHERS

———

ATRIA

New York London Toronto Sydney New Delhi

An Imprint of Simon & Schuster, LLC
1230 Avenue of the Americas
New York, NY 10020

First One Signal Publishers/Atria Books hardcover edition September 2024

ONE SIGNAL PUBLISHERS / ATRIA BOOKS and colophon are
trademarks of Simon & Schuster, LLC

Simon & Schuster: Celebrating 100 Years of Publishing in 2024

For information about special discounts for bulk purchases,
please contact Simon & Schuster Special Sales at 1-866-506-1949 or
business@simonandschuster.com.

The Simon & Schuster Speakers Bureau can bring authors to your
live event. For more information or to book an event, contact the
Simon & Schuster Speakers Bureau at 1-866-248-3049 or visit our website
at www.simonspeakers.com.

Interior design by Silverglass Design

Manufactured in the United States of America

1   3   5   7   9   10   8   6   4   2

Library of Congress Cataloging-in-Publication Data has been applied for.

ISBN 978-1-6680-7882-2
ISBN 978-1-6680-7884-6 (ebook)

For Plácido Arrue, Raúl Camacho, Salvador Zamorano,
Khammy Nothongkham, Alonso Rosa, Manuel Mandujano,
Jesús Lavato Molina, Martín Barroso, Martín Arenas,
Viensong Phanphengdee, and all the meatpacking
workers who died during the pandemic.

CONTENTS

PART II

7

AUTHOR'S NOTE
ON MORAL BEAUTY

Tyson Foods is the largest meat producer in the United States and is headquartered in my home state.

I grew up in the 1980s in rural Arkansas—the center of the meatpacking industry in America. The Ozark Mountains are home to a constellation of economically depressed towns like Oark, where I was born. My neighbors grew their own food and tried to make ends meet working odd jobs. Some, like my parents, raised and butchered chickens at home. After my dad and uncle (who lived across the dirt road) chopped off the chickens' heads, the birds would run around, their nerves briefly alive, as the last flows of life pulsed through their bodies. I close my eyes and see chickens running through the yard, their bloody heads left behind. Other people drove the forty-five miles to the chicken processing plant, where they worked and killed twelve thousand chickens per day, their hands in perpetual motion, completing a ritual both delicate and forceful—for one false movement could get them maimed or killed. In *The Jungle*, Upton Sinclair's 1906 novel about the meatpacking industry, he wrote of meatpacking workers, "They were willing to work all the time; and when people did their best, ought they not to be able to keep alive?" Over a century later, the question remains relevant.

In Oark, people canned vegetables from their garden, hunted deer and ducks, and spent summers swimming in the mineral blue lakes and rivers that dot the landscape. Some neighbors had it worse than others. In the 1970s, Mexicans and Central Americans arrived in the Ozarks searching for agricultural jobs that didn't pay much but allowed them to help their families back home—but only if the workers lived cheaply in Arkansas. When he first moved to Arkansas in the 1970s, Daniel Torres, an immigrant from Mexico, lived in an abandoned chicken house in the Ozark Mountains. By the time I was born in 1981, he had moved into a house built by my uncle Larry. With a big beard and a gentle way about him, Daniel became a part of my childhood, introducing me to my first Spanish words and Mexican hot chocolate. Whenever I biked up the hilly dirt road and crossed the Little Mulberry River, I would pass the chicken house where he had lived and imagine him huddled up in a corner, at the mercy of the elements, trying to sleep. As a child, I didn't question why he lived in an abandoned chicken house or what a detail like that might say about Arkansas and beyond. Like many migrants in the 1970s, Daniel had come from Mexico to Arkansas looking for work. He arrived in a state of lack, hoping to save money to send home. He got his start living in the abandoned chicken house. But he liked the Ozarks, the skies dark with stars and the woods teeming with rattlesnakes and copperheads. So he stayed.

Chicken farmers, squeezed by companies looking to extract maximum profits, often went out of business. What had once been a way to make a good living became cutthroat as a handful of companies controlled the market. The Arkansas landscape is marked by the poultry industry, by its decaying buildings that hint at the exploitation upon which meatpacking is modeled. At Walmart, an Arkansas-based global power and one of the few grocery stores within an hour of where I grew up, I would see immigrants with scarred wrists, infected hands, and missing fingers. Some of them were disabled and rode around the store in motorized carts. Their labor was invisible, but I could see the marks of it on their bodies.

....

In researching this book, I spent four years, from 2020 to 2024, interviewing dozens of current and former meatpacking workers at Tyson Foods and their family members. I began to investigate the meatpacking industry because I grew up around meatpacking workers and knew their stories. When the pandemic hit in March of 2020, I applied for funding from the National Geographic Society to write an article about the impact of COVID on the meatpacking industry. Confronting a powerful company worth billions was daunting, and I never imagined that what began as one article would become a book. However, as meatpacking workers began to die of COVID, I continued to interview their families, hoping that people were ready to listen.

It was challenging to conduct interviews during the early months of the pandemic. I also realized that by conducting interviews via phone, it would be difficult to build the trust necessary for workers to feel safe speaking about labor conditions at one of the wealthiest companies in the world. In September 2020, I began driving across Arkansas from one poultry town to the next, speaking to workers at their homes. I conducted interviews outside, observing social distancing. In November 2020, after conducting interviews in Springdale, I tested positive for COVID. I spent a month in bed as meatpacking workers, many of whom had survived COVID, texted me with advice. Sick with COVID and unable to work or earn money, I moved in with my parents. This was one of many moments when I believed I would not finish this project or support the workers in their quest for justice.

The people I interviewed lived with the stress of fearing they could lose their jobs if the company discovered they had spoken to a journalist. Many agreed to be interviewed only if their testimony was anonymous. At their request, I have changed their names and obscured identifying details to help maintain their privacy. The workers who did agree to be interviewed "on the record" and identify themselves by their first and last names are either dead or no longer work at Tyson Foods. All those involved in this project generously allowed me to accompany them as they went about their daily lives, and they hope their stories make the meatpacking industry safer. They shared painful, poetic, and mundane memories, sometimes at a significant cost to themselves. The interviews were conducted in Spanish, Marshallese, Karen, and English, and were recorded and transcribed for accuracy. I am bilingual and conducted most interviews in Spanish and translated them into English. Language is central to my work, and translation is a literary act.

To get a fuller picture of what happened during those years, workers provided documentation related to a class action lawsuit against Tyson Foods. These documents included medical files, letters, and financial information. Members of the lawsuit shared personal papers, videos, photos, and documents.

While Tyson Foods refers to workers as "team members," those interviewed did not want to be described with corporate language. In interviews, the workers wanted to discuss worker-led social movements and the power of a group of organized individuals to seek justice. I refer to them as they refer to themselves, as workers, organizers, and parents.

I am moved to do this work by what author C. E. Morgan describes as "moral beauty." In a 2016 interview, she said:

I think of moral beauty as what is the good and the just—terms perhaps best defined by their opposite: evil. Evil is the willingness to do damage to the other; its maximal expression is murder, but it includes a great deal of subtle and not-so-subtle injuries as it advances to that extreme. Evil acts reduce the other to an object, a being to its component parts, and obliterate subjectivity. Evil's breeding ground is a lack of empathy. So I locate moral beauty in an other-regarding ethic. Or perhaps it's better to say it's not *located* anywhere, because it's not a static entity. It's love, and love is not a feeling but an action.

This book explores the moral beauty of the immigrants who process our nation's meat and poultry, whose commitment to the good and the just is worthy of our attention.

PART I

1

WORKING IN THEIR SLEEP

I n the Ozark Mountains, copperheads mate in late summer, a tangle of thick reddish-brown bodies. Plácido Leopoldo Arrue thought their skin had a golden sheen when he saw them in the shade of his corn and tomato plants. His wife, Angelina Pacheco, picked the fruits of the garden planted with seeds from their home country, El Salvador. Angelina and Plácido's rental house in Springdale was built on land that was once home to the Osage Tribe. Like the original inhabitants of the Ozarks who planted corn in the same rocky soil, Angelina and Plácido were connected to the land by the food they grew.

Plácido died at the hospital on July 2, 2020. Angelina wanted justice for him. So she embarked on a quest to make sense of his life and death.

Plácido cut chicken at Tyson Foods. Some days, when he thought his wife and son couldn't hear, he cried in the bathroom before he got dressed. The house he and Angelina had rented for decades was a two-bedroom ranch on a street lined with houses in similar states of disrepair. The walls were thin, and neighbors could be heard speaking Spanish at a steady hum. Angelina planted rose bushes that lined the front of the house, and stray cats darted among them. Money was tight, but they managed to support their extended family in the US and El Salvador. Plácido wore Western shirts and liked to spend time with his seven children, sixteen grandchildren and one great-grandchild. He loved music, dancing, and gathering the family together for a meal.

As he left for his shift each afternoon at the nearby Tyson plant on Berry Street in Springdale, Plácido would walk from his bedroom through a room with a table covered in boxes of mangos, limes, cantaloupes, and oranges for the extended family who visited frequently. The room, though small, served as the entrance to the house as well as a dining room and a living room as it included a miniature sofa. Near the window, looking out to the street, was a small table flanked by a life-sized golden lamp with a spray of dangling pieces of polished glass. In the same room, on the wall facing the entry to the kitchen, was a large refrigerator.

Small, with low ceilings and peeling white paint, the kitchen was bathed in harsh fluorescent light. Like a tiny spaceship, the stove was covered in tinfoil to protect it from the hot oil Angelina used to fry empanadas. As she flattened a mass of dough between her palms, Angelina said that when she migrated to Arkansas, Plácido was good to her: "He paid the rent and bills. He liked to eat. He loved beef broth, beans with cheese, fried fish, and pupusas."

Leaving for work, Plácido would pass an apron hanging on a hook near the door above which hung a poster of a tiger's head, its teeth bared. Returning from work at four a.m., exhausted from a twelve-hour shift, Plácido would ask Angelina to rub his back until he fell asleep.

On summer nights, the house was humid and quiet except for the mournful sound of whip-poor-wills. Angelina lay next to her husband, her hair, long and dark, spread around her as she slept. She had been working at Tyson for several years when her nocturnal ritual began. Angelina's body was still except for her hands, which moved with surprising swiftness. They had memorized the movements, the exact strength it took to grip a knife, and the downward angle and force necessary to part flesh from bone. In her sleep, she drove the imaginary knife into the flesh between the chicken wing and body. Jerking down sharply to ensure a clean break, she then repeated the movement every three to five seconds, just as she did at the poultry processing plant.

Her hands moved against her will, gnarled as they were. With clenched fingers, she repeated the same disembodied motions. As if possessed, she worked through the night. Plácido sometimes found her hands moving like ghosts. In the mornings, Angelina woke up tired.

Barrel-chested, Plácido planted his garden in the rocky Arkansas soil each spring. In the front window of the house, he arranged river-worn stones. Plácido had worked since he was a child growing up in rural El Salvador. There was no money for him to attend school, so labor was all he knew. When he was in his late twenties, he migrated to the US alone in the 1990s to earn money to keep his wife and children back home fed and clothed. He set up a modest life in Arkansas and his family was able to join him.

Born in the rural Chilamate Valley in El Salvador, Angelina and her eleven siblings had also worked from a young age. Angelina lived in a rural area and, as a child, cut leaves from the garden to cover her feet. She didn't attend school and never learned to read. Her mom sewed her clothes out of pieces of shirts and skirts that belonged to her siblings. Her dad drank and hit Angelina. When she was twelve, she discovered she was pregnant by a thirty-year-old man and ran away from home with him.

Angelina met Plácido in her late twenties in rural El Salvador, where she lived with her three children and their father. One day, she was at the river washing clothes, her long, dark hair shining in the sun, when she looked up and locked eyes with Plácido. Both were in other relationships. "It shames me to say, but you can't tell the heart what to do," Angelina recalled. "We met, and it was love at first sight." They left their respective partners and their son, Darío, was born shortly after. It was then Plácido decided to migrate to the US—a journey that led him to Arkansas. Angelina followed him a few years later but left her children in El Salvador with their grandmother.

Plácido and Angelina, who both received work permits, married at the Fayetteville, Arkansas, courthouse on November 17, 1997. Angelina kept a copy of the marriage certificate in an envelope stuffed with important documents. Over the years, she and Plácido had received letters three times notifying them that they would be deported, but they were never deported and kept applying for and receiving work permits. Angelina's stories often had a timeless feel because she didn't know the why or when of events, and she couldn't refresh her memory by referring to letters, documents, or even Google. Whenever anyone had a question about dates or details, Angelina would hand them the envelope and let them look through the papers, allowing them to confirm information. But she didn't have a copy of the deportation letters and didn't know why she and Plácido had received them. To be illiterate is to rely on memory or, increasingly, on others.

....

Angelina and Plácido began working at Tyson Foods, the largest meatpacking company in the United States, the year the Twin Towers fell. Tyson Foods was founded in Springdale, Arkansas, in 1935 and is still headquartered there. It is the second largest global meatpacking company. It employs 141,000 people and operates 241 plants in the US, including facilities in twenty Arkansas communities. A Tyson facility is like a black hole, and nothing in town escapes the pull of the billion-dollar company. Tyson supplies grocery and restaurant chains like Arkansas-based Walmart, McDonald's, and Burger King, in addition to countless schools and prisons. In 2022, the company reported $53 billion in sales and produced one out of every five pounds of chicken, beef, and pork sold in America. Tyson is one of the top three meat suppliers to Walmart, and sales to Walmart account for about 18 percent of the meatpacking company's annual sales.

The meatpacking industry is dominated by a handful of companies like Tyson that wield extraordinary influence. The four largest meatpacking companies in the United States control 54 percent of the poultry market, 70 percent of the pork market, and 85 percent of the beef market. The companies reported record profits over the last decade, and have often lobbied to change state and federal laws and relax industry oversight. In 2021, Tyson reported a net income of approximately $3 billion, and, in 2020, a net income of $2 billion. In comparison, JBS, the largest meatpacking company in the world, reported $3.047 billion in net income in 2021. Despite such profits, industry wages have remained low for the industry's many immigrant workers. In 2021, poultry processing wages at Tyson Foods' plants in Arkansas put many workers at the poverty line, even as profits soared. Low wages didn't translate into lower prices for consumers, either.

Tyson builds its plants in small, rural towns, becoming the primary source of employment for residents, most of whom are immigrants. It's estimated that undocumented workers make up between 30 to 50 percent of the meatpacking workforce. Latinx workers like Plácido and Angelina make up 34.9 percent of the meatpacking workforce, greater than the percentage of African Americans, Whites, or Pacific Islanders employed. Meatpacking is one of the most dangerous jobs in the US, with an average of twenty-seven workers a day suffering amputation or hospitalization. For immigrants and refugees who have little schooling or are illiterate, it is one of the few jobs that pays above minimum wage.

Injury in the meatpacking industry can be slow and even boring, a series of interactions in which medical coverage is denied to a worker or a visit to a doctor is not approved. As companies like Tyson have shifted to using apps and artificial intelligence to interact with workers, the party responsible for disabling a worker has become nameless and faceless. While the bureaucratic inner workings of Tyson may seem too dull to be of interest, workers' lives hang in the balance.

Nothing is more American than meatpacking, an industry that employs almost 500,000 workers nationwide. But the US continues militarizing the border with Mexico and criminalizing immigration as though unaware of who plants, picks, and produces our nation's food. This immigration system, which makes immigrants' lives precarious, functions exactly as planned because workers who live in fear are easier to underpay, mistreat, and silence.

Workers at plants like Tyson are immigrants and refugees from all over the world, citizens and undocumented, literate and illiterate—making it harder for them to organize and band together. One individual plant can have workers from fifty countries who speak dozens of languages. What they have in common is the daily strength and endurance to work in conditions most would not tolerate.

Even with a steady supply of undocumented workers, Tyson has experienced labor shortages. In 2001, Tyson Foods was indicted by a federal grand jury for conspiracy to recruit illegal workers from Mexico and transport them to fifteen Tyson plants in nine states: Alabama, Indiana, Kentucky, Missouri, Mississippi, North Carolina, Tennessee, Texas, and Virginia.

The company blamed a few managers—Jimmy Rowland, a former Tyson manager at a plant in Shelbyville, Tennessee, among them. In April 2002, shortly after the federal government's indictment was made public, Rowland was found with a rifle wound to his chest. The coroner ruled it a suicide.

Tyson Foods representatives have discussed their management style, including in a May 2000 interview that was originally recorded for internal company use, Leland Tollett, who was the CEO at Tyson from 1991 to 1998 and interim CEO in 1999, admitted, "Our system, the way our business is run now, does not lend itself to the development of good general managers." He clarified that if managers kept costs down, "I could care less about how the guy does his job, how he accomplishes the tasks."

Government investigators said that two Tyson executives

knew the company was smuggling undocumented workers and helping them obtain counterfeit work documents. The case represented the largest in which Immigration and Naturalization Service had acted against a major American company for issues involving the smuggling of immigrants. However, in 2003, a federal jury acquitted Tyson and three managers of smuggling.

Employers like Tyson profit from hiring undocumented workers. The labor of undocumented workers underpins the national food system. In 2020, meat processing companies spent $4.1 million lobbying the US government. Between 2000 and 2021, for example, Tyson spent $25 million to block climate policies, decrease the chance of being inspected by the Occupational Safety and Health Administration (OSHA), and shield concentrated animal feeding operations from EPA fines.

In the interview, Tollett summed up how the company viewed immigrant and refugee workers. He said, "I think these people, these so-called immigrants, and we basically call them Hispanics because that is the biggest population in the workforce, I think they are learning the . . . I think they're learning the culture better, too." He also said that 1999 was the worst year at the company "in terms of death."

In the same internal company interview, Tollett said, "We would rather run a union-free environment because I think, you know, in the years we have convinced ourselves, took no convincing really, that our people are better off dealing with our company. We are fair people. And if we're not fair to people in something, we need to figure out how to make sure that those people do understand that we're trying to be fair."

While the average Tyson line worker might make as little as $22,000 a year, an associate director at the corporate office could make over $150,000. In that same May 2000 internal interview, Buddy Wray, who served as president of Tyson from 1991 to 2000 and was on the board of directors from 1994 to 2003, said of immigrant line workers, "Without those employees from other countries that don't speak English we'd be out of business. The percentage of Hispanics and the percentage of other nationalities that we hire today are just increasing every year, and I don't see that changing." Wray wasn't worried about foreign workers assimilating to the US because "We brought Black people here that could not speak English from Africa. And they were the people working in the South. And in the North, we had Italians, and we had Irish, and we had Europeans, which a lot of them didn't speak English, the Chinese in the West. So, we don't have anything different today than we had in the early 1800s. And time will resolve that."

This view of cheap labor was widespread in Arkansas and transcended party lines. Bill and Hillary Clinton used prison labor in the Governor's Mansion in Little Rock when they lived there in the 1980s and 1990s. In *It Takes a Village*, Hillary Clinton noted that staffing their residence with prison labor was "a longstanding tradition, which kept costs down."

Similarly, in addition to employing undocumented workers, Tyson also exploits vulnerable prison populations. For example, some nonviolent criminals facing jail time in Oklahoma are offered an alternative to prison—they can attend programs like the Northeastern Oklahoma Council on Alcoholism or Freedom from Addiction through Christ. For many people facing prison time, even those who aren't alcoholics or addicts, a recovery program seems like a better option than prison. However, those who know the programs call them "the Chicken Farm" as they require people to work at Tyson or other meatpacking companies, where they are paid little or nothing. Tyson, which presents itself publicly as a Christian company and often employs religious language or imagery to describe its work, has made lucrative partnerships with religious rehab programs that provide a pipeline of low-paid workers.

Tyson's ubiquity in American life grants its owners extraordinary political power. For decades, the company has exploited weakened antitrust regulations to acquire smaller companies and facilities, like Cassady Broiler Company and Cobb-Vantress. In doing so, Tyson has exercised an outsized influence in Arkansas in ways that wielded its growing influence to increase profits by putting workers at risk. Over the past thirty years, as Tyson has increasingly exploited the immigrants, incarcerated people, and children who toil in its factories, shareholder profits have soared.

Tyson has been innovative and aggressive in creating programs to employ vulnerable populations. In 2023, Arkansas made it easier to employ children. Although legislators framed the law as an opportunity to provide children with work experience and a work ethic, immigrant children leave the premises when the shifts change at some Tyson plants in Arkansas. In February 2023, the US Department of Labor announced that more than 100 children were illegally employed in hazardous jobs across the US, including six children working at a Tyson facility in Green Forest, Arkansas.

The lack of protections for meatpacking workers is a product of long-standing bipartisan inaction in addressing labor rights in the industry. During the 1992 presidential election, Ross Perot called Bill Clinton, then the governor of Arkansas, "chicken man," a reference to his close relationship with

Donald Tyson, the former head of Tyson Foods who was a driving political force during Clinton's time in Little Rock. As the governor of Arkansas, Clinton oversaw lax regulations on the meatpacking industry, leading to the contamination of drinking water and hundreds of miles of rivers and streams.

Democrat ties to Big Ag did not end with Clinton. Tom Vilsack, agriculture secretary during the Obama administration and again under President Joe Biden, pushed poultry plants to increase their slaughter line speeds and passed off specific government inspection duties to meatpacking employees. In *The Meat Racket*, author Christopher Leonard argues that the Obama administration also gave into lobbying and continued business as usual rather than taking on the abuses in the meat industry.

During the Trump administration, poultry lobbyists representing companies like the Arkansas-based chicken purveyor Mountaire continued to hold significant sway over lawmaking. Ronald Cameron, the owner and chairman of Mountaire, donated nearly $3 million to organizations supporting Trump's candidacy. This later contributed to lax oversight of how such companies protected and paid workers during the COVID pandemic.

Further, the US government spends more than $30 billion annually in federal funding to agribusiness. By subsidizing the meatpacking industry, the government ensures that American consumers are not faced with the actual cost of meat nor forced to reckon with the realities of how the meatpacking industry contributes to climate change. Taxpayer-funded farm subsidies support the meatpacking industry by aiding corn and soybean farms, crops frequently used for animal feed production.

Despite these subsidies, companies like Tyson still rely on

the exploitation of workers like Angelina and Plácido to keep prices low and increase their corporate profits. As Eyal Press discusses in *Dirty Work: Essential Jobs and the Hidden Toll of Inequality in America*, "Both on the right and on the left, then, albeit for very different reasons, the people working in America's slaughterhouses are likely to be viewed disparagingly. To be seen as dirty, which is how people whose jobs bring them into direct contact with the flesh and blood of animals have long been seen in many cultures."

2

SAFE WORK

On their way to the Tyson plant on Berry Street in Springdale, Angelina and Plácido would drive past a series of banners touting the company's safety record, including one that read, "Safe work is the only work at Tyson." From the road, they could see Tyson Foods semitrailers covered in advertisements for crispy strips—giant-sized pieces of breaded chicken floating on a red background. Angelina and Plácido would pass through an authorization point titled "Team Member Entrance" to reach the employee parking lot inside the expansive fenced property.

Once they entered the plant, they were required to leave their phones and other belongings in a common area—workers hung their backpacks or purses on hooks. The state Ag-Gag law prohibits workers and visitors from taking photos, videos, or audio recordings inside the plant. However, meatpacking companies framed this as an effort to protect trade secrets. Six states have ag-gag laws, including Arkansas, which authorizes farms and businesses like Tyson to sue for as much as $5,000 per day if a person records audio or video inside company installations. Plácido and Angelina would put on white aprons made of chicken feathers, which were woven into a fabric that looked like synthetic material—the company wasted nothing. Tyson also made the workers' hairnets out of feathers, which workers said looked like any other hairnet but smelled terrible.

Then the workers picked out safety equipment, hoping they could find what they needed in the correct size. OSHA is the national agency that oversees health and safety in the meatpacking industry. It requires meatpacking companies like Tyson to provide workers with personal protective equipment, including helmets, steel mesh gloves, wrist and forearm guards, waterproof aprons, footwear with nonslip soles, hearing protection, and goggles. Any power tools the workers used needed safety guards and shutoff switches, and each worker's knife needed to be sharp and have guards to prevent the hand holding the knife from slipping over the blade. However, Tyson did not have a system to provide workers with equipment that fit. Plácido and Angelina competed against their co-workers daily to get protective gear in the correct size, a grim game that someone lost every day, potentially to their peril.

Tyson plants are sprawling facilities, often between 100,000 and 300,000 square feet, with stunning, bleeding, scalding, defeathering, evisceration, and carcass-chilling areas. Live chickens are delivered and killed in the open air; consequently, those areas are subject to the weather. The parts of the plant where the carcass is divided up, packaged, and chilled are cold or below freezing. Much of the work is mechanized, and the high noise levels endured by the workers over the years can cause hearing damage. The smell of the hundreds of thousands of chickens slaughtered each day wafts out of the plant, blanketing small towns with the ripe odor of rotting meat and chicken poop. Inside, line workers toil under a flood of fluorescent lights doing repetitive motion work for eight- to ten-hour shifts. Between the chilling of poultry and the nightly sanitation of work areas, facilities are host to a menagerie of hazardous chemicals. Sanitation workers, often contracted via a third party so Tyson can avoid liability for accidents, work at night, typically for twelve-hour shifts. A 2023 investigation by the *New York Times* found minors working in sanitation at some Tyson plants.

At the Tyson plant in Springdale, Plácido and Angelina soon discovered that even walking was a challenge. Plant floors are covered in a mixture of the oil used for frying, the mucus that clings to chicken, frozen bits of chicken, and blood. Even entering the cafeteria was like walking on Crisco. Plácido and Angelina had to brace their entire bodies and walk deliberately to avoid falling. It took them some time to understand the plant layout and the killing process.

Tyson employs a vertically integrated model in which they control every aspect of animal production (breeder flock, pullet farm, breeder house, hatchery, broiler farm, processing, and distribution). The process begins at chicken houses owned by small and independent farmers contracted by Tyson. The chicken houses are an average of thirty-four miles from the poultry processing facility they supply. On any night, entering the chicken houses spread around rural Arkansas, you can find young men, some of them fourteen- or fifteen-year-old immigrant children, grabbing up to four chickens in each hand to cage them. With mechanical ferocity, they hurl roughly eighty chickens into each cage, and then the cages are loaded onto a semitrailer.

This is how poultry processing begins, when the chickens are sleeping—although as soon as the birds become aware of the catchers, they peck and scratch furiously, digging into the catchers' flesh. The catchers wear long-sleeved shirts and pants but lack protective gear. They breathe in the sharp smell of ammonia as well as dust that contains manure, feed, and feathers. These children make around $2.25 for every thousand chickens, money many of them give to their parents. In 2023, two indigenous immigrant minors from Guatemala who worked as catchers requested support from an Arkansas-based poultry workers' labor rights organization. The underage workers wanted to recover unpaid wages from a Tyson supplier. The children, who spoke only their indigenous language, had been working sixteen-hour days.

After the Tyson semitrailer drivers pick up cages of chickens from nearby farms, the drivers head to the plant in Springdale. They park their trucks near the open-air killing area, which is only covered with a metal roof. In the summer, where temperatures often rise above one hundred degrees, workers kill the chickens in the sweltering heat; while in the winter, they work in the cold. No matter the weather, they wear yellow raincoats, boots, and gloves to minimize their contact with chicken blood, fecal matter, and guts. To prevent contamination between the live kill area and the chicken processing area, each area has its own cafeteria and bathrooms.

The plant workers in Springdale unload the cages and manually pull the birds out to put them on the "live hang." They have two seconds to grab the incoming chickens out of the cages and hang them by their feet. At some plants, the process has been mechanized, and a machine picks up a cage of chickens and places it on a conveyor belt that delivers the chickens to workers in "live hang." But not at the Springdale plant, where—wearing rubber boots, aprons, hairnets, face masks, and gloves—the workers fight to hang resistant chickens. Due to the ungodly speed of work, men often urinate in corners in the live hang area where there is less oversight.

A breast rub machine calms the chickens with an electric pulse before they are stunned. Entering the "kill room," a machine slits their throats. Workers known as "backup killers" prod chickens, their aprons splattered with blood. If any birds are still alive, they slice their necks again. Looking down, workers say they see their faces reflected in a pool of blood.

The defeathering room is where the headless chickens are bathed in boiling water and then plucked clean by mechanical fingers. To automate as much work as possible, Tyson opened a Manufacturing Automation Center in 2019 near its headquarters in Springdale. The facility develops automated and robotic solutions for plants nationwide.

Mechanical claws extract livers, gizzards, and hearts in the evisceration department. The company was at a loss for years about what to do with the gizzards since customers weren't fond of them. In the early 1990s, Tyson began to sell gizzard patties to prisons. Don Tyson, the company's chairman at the time, described imprisoned people as a "captive market" for gizzard burgers. Another machine cuts off chicken feet, which workers wash and package, mainly for export to China. Workers stand on wet mesh platforms to avoid the wastewater canal of water and blood running through their area. One false step and they could slip and injure themselves.

At this point, the chicken enters the refrigerated side of the plant, where most tasks require human hands, including Angelina's and Plácido's. Workers must react quickly because the line speed is set by supervisors, but the workers say they are not told in advance when the line speed changes. In the debone area, workers use brute force to shove chickens on steel cones that move down the line flanked by cutters. With a knife in one hand and a stainless-steel wire metal glove on the other, workers take two to five seconds to slice off the wings. Farther down the line, others remove breasts and the meat for chicken nuggets. Angelina and Plácido quickly learned that a live chicken could be killed, gutted, cut, and processed into chicken breasts, nuggets, or patties within a few hours.

They described the jobs of other Tyson workers, the small tasks that made up a day: carrying bags of salt to mix into nuggets and other products, washing poop off chicken feet, opening boxes of frozen chicken with a crowbar, and picking up pieces of chicken off the floor that would later be converted into dog food.

. . . .

On weekends, if Plácido wasn't working, he liked fishing and exploring the rivers in the area. Whatever he caught, he would bring home to Angelina, who would fry the fish to make pupusas. Arkansas surprised them, mainly because they had never heard anything about the state before arriving. The northwest corner where they lived was mountainous, and minerals had turned its rivers blue and green. They felt connected to the land and wanted to make the small plot they rented their own and grow food as they had done in El Salvador.

At Tyson, Plácido met Martín, who lived within minutes of his house. Martín woke every day at four a.m. to prepare for work, entering the Berry Street Plant before the production lines began to run. For $13 an hour he packed chicken feet: he made boxes, got ice, and stacked the boxes. A father of seven from Guadalajara, Mexico, Martín Barroso migrated to the US in 1986 and received amnesty. He later arranged for his wife and children to join him in 2001.

Martín often complained about a foot that bothered him. His son, Gabriel, said, "At work, he entered early and gathered the boxes, went to the freezer to get ice, made the boxes, and when production began, he had to put the boxes on the pallet, stack boxes, and take them to the freezer." Despite the physically challenging work, Gabriel described his father as "always happy." Gabriel said, "When there was a party, he was happy. He wasn't ever in a bad mood. He was a good person, friendly to everyone, and had no problem with anyone."

Gabriel worked at Tyson from 2011 to 2017. He spent nine months in debone and then five more years as a line supervisor in the debone department, where the whole chicken is cut into pieces: legs, shoulders, breast, wings, and feet. His wife worked in poultry processing at an Arkansas-based poultry company that is among the top ten chicken producers in the US.

At Tyson, Plácido also became friends with Víctor, who like Martín, had migrated to Arkansas from Mexico. Víctor and his wife lived in a ranch-style house in Springdale, within ten miles of Plácido's and Martín's, and their house is decorated with portraits of Pope John Paul II and the Virgin of Guadalupe. Víctor began working at the Berry Street Plant in the debone area cutting chicken shoulders. When Víctor wasn't working and the weather was nice, he would sit in his backyard.

Born in Irapuato, Víctor grew up in a family of farmers. His grandfather, Jesús, who lived in the same town, planted corn and wheat, as did his father, Margarito. In 1997, when Víctor was fifteen, his parents migrated with their five children to the US. Margarito told him simply that they were looking for a better life. They chose Arkansas because Víctor's dad had friends who worked in the meatpacking industry who had told him, "In Arkansas, there is always work." Unlike in Arizona, where jobs were seasonal—picking lemons or oranges—meatpacking jobs were year-round. At first, Víctor's parents got jobs at the Butterball turkey processing plant in Huntsville, twenty-eight miles east of Springdale, where his father works to this day. His mother got a job at Tyson working in debone.

After finishing high school, Víctor worked in construction for a decade before finding a job at George's poultry plant. In 1999, while processing chicken at George's, he met his wife, Gloria. An immigrant from El Salvador with a heart-shaped face and dimples, she made him laugh. Gloria thought she would save money and return to El Salvador, but in 2003 she and Víctor married and began to make a life in Arkansas. Although she missed El Salvador and he dreamed of Mexico, they began to explore the Ozark Mountains and the rivers and lakes surrounding Springdale. In 2000, one of Víctor's friends told him that the work at Tyson was easy and paid $11/hour. "And he convinced me, and I went and applied and got work," said Víctor. Both he and Gloria began to work at Tyson in the early 2000s. That's how Víctor learned that Tyson provided employees who referred friends with a $2,000 to $4,000 referral bonus.

Víctor received medical insurance through Tyson that covered his children, which was why he stayed at the job. After two decades at the company, he explained, "I get three weeks of paid vacation, and if I start over, I won't have anything. Many people have already worked for fifteen to twenty years and have a month of vacation. They have a 401(k), and that is why they don't leave. People endure being there and don't leave."

Gloria was twenty-one when she migrated to Arkansas from San Miguel, El Salvador, with an aunt. She said, "There was no work in El Salvador. My family was in the US, and they decided I should join them." She has worked at Tyson's Berry Street Plant in Springdale for over two decades in the evisceration department— the area with live chickens. It was hot because of the baths of scalding water used to clean the chickens after they were killed. "The chicken passes by," she explained, "and the chicken doesn't have feathers, but it is still whole. No head, no feet, but it is whole. I open the chicken with scissors when the machine can't open it, and then it passes through a machine that takes out the guts."

The heat presented an extra challenge for workers in Gloria's area because they needed to drink water to avoid dehydration, but, as a result, they had to go to the bathroom more frequently. Supervisors often denied workers bathroom breaks because they needed them to reach their daily production quotas. For each eight-hour shift, Tyson employees were required to have a thirty-minute lunch break and two twenty-minute breaks. However, workers complained that breaks were shortened since the time it took them to take off and put on all their protective equipment was included in the break. Derek Burleson, the director of public relations, said that some plants allow workers one thirty-minute unpaid break or more per eight-hour shift, while others have two breaks of more than 20 minutes.

When Gloria started working at Tyson, she and others in her area wore plastic gloves, but workers sometimes cut themselves and got blood on the chicken. Eventually, Tyson provided them with steel mesh metal gloves.

Gloria would enter the Berry Street Plant at 4:38 a.m. each morning. Once inside, she would hang her belongings on a hook. On her line, she would cut open chickens with scissors. A machine was supposed to cut them, but it only worked sometimes. The chickens traveled on a conveyor belt from her line to a machine that pulled their guts out. "They don't tell us if the lines are slow or fast," she said, noting that there was an office where managers could check line speeds, but workers weren't allowed to enter. She said the faster the line speed, the more accidents workers experienced, noting that a man she knew had recently lost several fingers working where they hang live chickens.

At seven a.m., Gloria would take a ten-minute break to go to the bathroom: "They pay for the bathroom break because it's only ten minutes," Gloria said. When she first began working at Tyson, workers were only allowed one ten-minute bathroom break per eight-hour shift. However, since that rule caused workers to pee on themselves or resort to wearing diapers, it was changed so that workers could request permission from their supervisors to go to the bathroom more than once. At 8:40 a.m., she would punch out for thirty unpaid minutes to eat breakfast. At eleven a.m., she would take another bathroom break. By one p.m., she would head home. Monday through Friday, that was her schedule.

When Gloria gave birth to her children, Tyson paid her $800 during her four weeks of maternity leave.

Line workers like Gloria spent years working in one area of the plant, and their knowledge of the company was often limited. "I don't know how they grow and feed chickens," admitted

Gloria. She lamented that the USDA hadn't visited her plant in three years, and she continued to see rotten chicken. Gloria said, "You see everything bad. They don't want to waste any chicken."

Although workers wanted to organize to improve labor conditions and oversight at the plant, Gloria said, "They won't let us organize. The truth is people are afraid." Workers endured it all because they were frightened of losing their jobs. "They have all the power here. Tyson can buy people or anything they need," said Gloria. When the media published articles about Tyson's labor practices, Gloria said the company responded by investigating which employees had spoken to the media. "The only thing that bothers them is when workers speak with reporters," Gloria said.

Tyson's managers constantly told workers they could trust their supervisors with anything—that the company would help them. But Víctor and Gloria did not have that experience. "It is to fake you out, so it seems they help," Gloria said. "Anything that happens in the plant, they warn all the other plants and prohibit us from speaking to the media. Like the decapitation."

On March 3, 2020, Carlos Lynn, thirty-nine, was sanitizing a fifty-foot chicken chiller at a Tyson plant in Baker Hill, Alabama. Lynn, a Black man from Alabama, worked for Packers Sanitation Services Inc., which paid formerly incarcerated men like him $12–$15/hour to do dangerous sanitation work. The chicken chiller is essentially an ice bath for chicken. While cleaning the chiller, Lynn's head was caught at a pinch point where a moving blade passes close to a stationary object or other moving part. The machine was somehow turned on while Lynn was inside; however, Tyson did not have cameras recording activity in the area. The resulting investigation showed that the chicken chiller was missing a safety guard that was required by federal law. However, because Tyson hired Lynn via a third-party service, the company took no responsibility for Lynn's death.

The following day, supervisors at Gloria's plant in Springdale warned workers not to respond to media requests about the decapitation. Then, Gloria said that the plant required all workers to sign a legal document stating that they understood the risks of sanitizing the chicken chiller, and, if they were decapitated, they accepted responsibility for such an accident since they had been warned of the risk beforehand. The document was in English.

....

Rosario, who met Gloria and Víctor at work at Tyson, was born in San José Ixtapa, Guerrero, Mexico, in 1973. Her face is pale and round, luminous like the moon, and her eyes are green and flecked with brown. Her voice is low and calming, just above a whisper. Her hands, swollen from cutting chicken wings, sometimes move against her wishes, just like Angelina's. Short and stout, Rosario wears her wavy blond hair, which is darker at the roots, long and tightly pulled back.

Rosario migrated to the US in 1995, when she was twenty-one, because she wanted to get a job and send her family money. She crossed the border into Arizona and from there traveled to Rogers, Arkansas, where she had family. Devoutly religious, she prayed for migrants daily. Rogers, eleven miles from Springdale, in the state's mountainous northwest corner, is the home of the first Walmart store, which opened on July 2, 1962. The center of town features brick-lined streets with a mix of local stores, the original Walmart, and the Tyson Chick-N-Quick Plant. In recent years, the salaries of corporate personnel at Tyson and Walmart have turned the town center into an expensive and coveted area to raise children. On August 9, 2009, Rosario started working at the plant in Springdale for $7/hour. She was assigned to the debone area, where she cut chicken wings with a knife for eight hours a day. Rosario said, "They increase the line speed a lot. Cutting chicken ruins your hands." When she saved up enough money, she wanted to go to beauty school and open her own salon.

Early in her shift, Rosario sometimes needed to go to the bathroom, but she never knew if her supervisor would give her permission. A "yes" was just the beginning. Rosario knew her time was limited, but she was afraid to run for fear of slipping on the chicken sludge on the floor. No matter how fast she walked, she could hear the heavy breathing of her supervisor following closely behind her. Reaching the bathroom, she had only a few moments before the supervisor would shout from the doorway of the women's restroom, "Why are you taking so long?" Like many women at the plant, Rosario experienced frequent urinary tract infections because of the line supervisors' scrutiny: "Even the break, they don't want to give it to you." Breaks, whether mandated by law or necessitated by the call of nature, lowered production.

Rosario worked elbow to elbow with Gloria on the debone line, holding knives and scissors. Given the speed of the work, injuries were common. Rosario learned, "If you cut yourself, sometimes you remain silent. If you get help, they treat you bad and marginalize you. It isn't your fault because they don't provide the necessary supplies. Sometimes, they give you gloves that are too big."

In her first few weeks of work, Rosario witnessed a co-worker cut herself deeply. The only steel mesh glove available that morning was too large for her co-worker and had slipped off her hand.

Rosario said of Tyson's supervisors, "They told her that she had to sign a document accepting that the accident was her fault. They force you to sign it when they are to blame for negligence. They don't check on safety supplies. They don't count safety equipment to ensure the correct supplies for workers. They always blame the worker. After hearing it so much, we came to believe it. But they are the ones who are negligent—not us. The workers know—it is Tyson. OSHA does nothing."

In theory, OSHA inspects meatpacking facilities to ensure that they are following safety regulations and responds to workplace fatalities and worker complaints. In practice, OSHA has been consistently underfunded and understaffed, often leaving meatpacking companies to police themselves. In 2020, the meatpacking industry spent $4.1 million on lobbying. For years, this money contributed to the necessary bipartisan agreement to starve OSHA. Underfunded and understaffed for decades, the organization rarely fines meatpacking companies for labor violations, and when they do, the fines are low enough to encourage the continued violation of labor rights. In 2019, OSHA inspected fewer than one-half of 1 percent of the companies it regulated.

. . . .

Tall and stout, with a face that rarely betrayed emotion, Mateo worked with Rosario, Víctor, and Gloria at the Berry Street Plant as a line worker and later as a team leader. Born in Guanajuato, Mexico, he arrived in the US as a child. Because he received citizenship, he talked about how he hadn't faced the same difficulties as workers like Rosario and Plácido. Mateo oversaw a line where workers packed the breaded and cooked chicken products. He began work at the plant picking up condemned chicken, "the stuff that falls on the floor." He threw the chicken scraps into yellow barrels labeled "condemned."

Quetzali lived some forty-five minutes from the plant where Mateo worked. She had migrated to the US from San Marcos, Guatemala, in 1998 and ended up in Green Forest. To get to Green Forest from Springdale, you drive nearby the Boston Mountains, which are more like hills, past Eureka Springs, toward a town whose central architecture involves acres of meatpacking facilities, including a hatchery. With less than three thousand people, most of the city works at Tyson or in jobs related to the industry. One main street runs through the town, taking you by the Tyson complex. The surrounding area is covered in eastern cottonwoods, willows, and green ash trees.

Quetzali's house is a few streets from the Tyson plant where she worked, down a dirt road that dead-ended into an overgrown property with large signs all around that said, "no photos," "no surveillance," and "no trespassing." The house was small and dark with two bedrooms, a living room, and a kitchen connected to a garage. She and her husband had rented the house for over two decades, paying around $400 monthly to the owner who worked in management at Tyson. A cross hung on the porch.

In Green Forest, Quetzali found work cutting chicken for Tyson at one of their largest plants in Arkansas. First, she worked in slaughter, then in packing, and finally in white meat debone, where she cut wings for $17.50 an hour, ten hours a day, four to five days a week. She divided her time at Tyson into her undocumented years working under a fake name and her documented years working under her real one. On weekends, she went to thrift stores and yard sales, buying used clothes by the box, which she stored in her garage and the room next to her bedroom. She sent the boxes via bus to her mother's house in La Blanca, and her mother sold the clothes. Quetzali wanted to help support her mother financially, "I call her every day, and we talk. I tell her I'm ok. I don't want her to get depressed because she knows I am sick."

The hands of any worker tell you a story, one of missing fingers and scars, deep and textured like a dry riverbed. At bedtime, when Quetzali got sleepy, her hands jumped, just like Angelina's and Rosario's did. She had been cutting chicken at a Tyson plant in Green Forest for over two decades. Quetzali's hands often went numb in moments when she needed them most, a sign of carpal tunnel syndrome. Tyson's on-site nurses listened to Quetzali's worries, giving her ice and sending her back to work. Soon she began working in her sleep, grabbing chicken breasts and cutting them with scissors. Sometimes, she woke up covered in scratches. Worried, she went to a doctor who told her she had little control over her nerves. She said, "The doctor gave me a cast for my hands, but it's not plaster. It's like a hard glove." The doctor told her to wear the gloves at night.

Quetzali is a short, powerful woman, her face round and expressive. Her hands are often clenched, her fingers curled against her will, a side effect of years of repetitive-motion labor. Her face and hands are inflamed from not only the repetitive work but also the resulting cocktail of medications she takes daily. "The body has a memory," she said. "You can't rest because the trauma remains in the body."

Quetzali became a US resident after she married her husband, Bobby, a Texan. She met him at the plant in 2000, where he worked washing the box lids from the reusable plastic containers that were used to store newly processed chicken before it was put in the freezer. He was thirty-two years her senior and divorced with grown children. They married in 2009 and didn't have children. On the wall of their home, above the couch hang two plaques, gold nameplates on wooden bases commemorating the first decade she and her husband worked at Tyson, alongside three photos of their wedding and a painting of the Last Supper. Quetzali said, "He likes to drink beer and buy meat. He lives in the moment. He said, 'I don't want to buy a house because my kids will take it from you when I die. Better to eat the money.'" In their wedding photo, which hangs above a small dining table, they are dressed in old-time Texan formal wear. Quetzali, sitting on a bench before a piano, is dressed in white silk and a matching white hat. Her husband, wearing a black suit and matching bowler hat, stands at her side, his left hand resting on a cane.

When Quetzali first began working at Tyson in 2000, nobody questioned her fake social security card. But Quetzali worried because a friend told her that Tyson could expose her anytime and have her deported if she did something the company didn't like. After years of fearing that Tyson would retaliate against her for her undocumented status, she was thankful to her husband because "he helped me get my residency." When she became a resident, management at the plant issued her a new work ID under her real name without asking her any questions.

Tyson and other meatpacking companies rely on the Immigration and Reform Control Act of 1986. While the act made hiring undocumented immigrants illegal, it also acknowledged that employers weren't document experts. Because workers like Quetzali had to fill out an I-9 form declaring under penalty of perjury that they were authorized to work, it was easy for companies like Tyson to retaliate against workers. Conversely,

Tyson could choose to not make trouble if they wanted to keep the worker—as long as the worker admitted that, while they once weren't a resident, now they were.

Quetzali was diagnosed with breast cancer in early 2019. Her doctor gave her a note stating she should be allowed to go to the bathroom at work whenever she needed to. Even then, she said, her supervisor would follow her to the stall and ask her loudly, as she emerged, why she had taken so long. "It is a psychological game," she said, of how supervisors treated workers.

When Quetzali complained to her supervisor about another worker trying to put his hand between her butt cheeks, as if her pants were no obstacle, the supervisor said, "you are all my children," and did nothing about it. Quetzali's co-worker continued to sexually harass her.

The pandemic only increased such dynamics, given the fear of COVID combined with the pressure to keep production up. During the pandemic, the company, desperate for workers, pressured them to work extra days. More than living in Arkansas, they lived inside the nation of Tyson—they spent more time with chicken nuggets, feet, and patties than with their children.

Margarita, a close friend of Quetzali's at the Green Forest Tyson Plant, was born in San Marcos, Guatemala, and migrated to the US, where she received political asylum. Faintly pink roses grew in her yard, and her house was newly painted. Her living room was decorated with photos of her children, including one of her daughter in a billowing quinceañera dress.

She had spent almost three decades at Tyson, half the time cutting chicken wings and the other half bagging. In the first years of cutting wings, she got used to putting on the cloth, plastic, and steel mesh glove over one hand and the difficulty of sharpening her knife between cutting wings. A dull blade could be dangerous, but to sharpen the knife between cutting wings was also a situation ripe for accidents. Of her work bagging chicken, she said, "I make the boxes and have them ready. I grab five bags of chicken and throw them in the box." Each bag weighed eight pounds, and she packed them for ten hours a day.

Margarita said of the faint scar across her palm, "*Que esto se llama carpal tunnel.*" The problem with Tyson, she said, is "they want high production and to look good and for the workers to kill themselves."

3

THE CHICKEN
NUGGETS RECIPE

In March 2017, Víctor applied for a higher-paying position at Tyson's Chick-N-Quick Plant in Rogers, where he began to work as a machine operator. His shift ran from two to eleven p.m. One day, he sat in a plastic chair in his backyard in Springdale as his youngest son ran around with an umbrella. Víctor leaned back in his chair. "All the waste from the debone area, the skeleton, the skin, the neck, the hip bone—all of that is ground up to make nuggets which have almost no meat in them," he said. Nuggets, a product Tyson created for McDonald's, helped transform Tyson from a small-town business into a global empire.

The nugget recipe involved forty-pound frozen blocks of chicken parts: three blocks of chicken breast; two of ground skeleton mixed with blood, necks, and other bits; and one of chicken skin and fat. Víctor began his shift by using a crowbar to open the frozen boxes of chicken parts. In his experience, "Many times, the chicken is rotten. It smells. It arrives like a rock. When we open it, it is already a different color, not pink. It is green or purple."

Sitting in the yard, a scream rung out, and Víctor's youngest daughter came running into the backyard, her right eye dripping blood. "He poked me in the eye with the umbrella," she said, pointing to her little brother, who stood barefoot, eyes wide, in a diaper and t-shirt. Víctor sat in his chair and told her, "When I was a child, I got gored by a bull." Crying, she ran back into the house.

With hardly a pause, Víctor continued to describe how to make chicken nuggets. At work, he dumped the forty-pound blocks of chicken parts into a large grinder and added salt, preservatives, and flavors. Watching the blocks go into the grinder, Víctor often wondered how much cardboard people ate in their nuggets. The chicken arrived at the nugget room in frozen blocks inside the cardboard boxes. The boxes had no plastic liner, so the frozen chicken stuck to the cardboard when workers pried the blocks out of the boxes. Víctor reported an instance in which a metal crowbar fell into the nuggets grinder and they had to stop the line to clean the grinder. He noted that "anything could be in there." He said of the nuggets, "If we take the time to remove all the cardboard, the line doesn't have chicken. And the supervisor will say, 'Why are you taking so long?'"

The cardboard boxes are piled in stacks on the wet floor. They are opened to reveal the raw meat inside, the floor strewn with bits of chicken from the endless process of opening boxes. Workers, covered from head to toe in safety equipment, looking more like blobs than humans, push around large plastic carts filled with the frozen blocks of meat. Although the space is cavernous, it is simultaneously claustrophobic as the ceiling is covered with pipes and the floor is an obstacle course of heavy machinery, work lines with knives and scissors, and people running like worker bees from one point to another with industrial volumes of chicken.

After the nuggets are formed, they are bathed in butter, bread-crumbs, and flour. Víctor was disgusted when bags of flour were full of weevils, complaining about the weevils contaminating the nuggets. Once breaded, the nuggets went into the fryer for one minute, just enough to fry the breaded part—not the meat. They were then steamed and put in the freezer for twenty-five to thirty minutes, after which they came out like little rocks.

....

According to Tyson Foods, the company's success is the simple story of a rural boy looking for opportunity in small-town Arkansas.

In the 1940s, John W. Tyson, the founder of the family business, bought a broiler farm in Springdale and began crossbreeding chickens to produce a higher meat yield, which later became standard practice in the industry. When John incorporated Tyson Feed and Hatchery in 1947, he provided the model for a vertically integrated company that controls different stages along the supply chain. The company would supply chicks to farmers, sell feed to farmers, and transport chickens to market.

In 1952, when John's son, Don, was twenty-two, Don dropped out of college and became the general manager of his father's company. Don, short and paunchy with a wide grin, was as well-known for working hard as he was for partying and surrounding himself with young women. He often said, "I don't have time to have a bad time."

In 1953, the Arkansas General Assembly adopted the nickname "The Land of Opportunity," a nod to an unfettered pro-business environment where unions weren't welcome. The lack of regulations in the state allowed the company to take risks, ones that came at the expense of workers. In 1954, with growing profits, the Tyson family began contributing money to political campaigns across the state. Over the coming decades, company-backed political candidates governed Arkansas and even the nation.

Don worked with Leland Tollett and Donald Wray, known as Buddy. Tollett and Wray first met in the summer of 1955 at Southern State College (now Southern Arkansas University). They later transferred to the University of Arkansas. Tollett, who had an innocent look and the coiffed hair of a Southern preacher, began working at Tyson Feed and Hatchery in 1959 as the director of research and nutrition. Wray started as a field representative at the company in 1961. As it grew, the Tyson family and the powerful executives they hired focused on hiring friends and those they saw as sharing the same values.

In the 2000 internal interview, Buddy described how he conducted interviews to see if people were morally aligned with the company. He said, "We ask open-ended questions, and you don't break any laws that way, you know, really breaking any laws that way. What did your mother do? She worked here, and he worked there. Are they separated? So, you don't have to come right out and ask what kind of home life they had."

By 1966, John had named his son, Don, president of the company. In 1967, John Tyson and his wife were killed when their car was hit by a train. Don took over as CEO of the family business, and Tollett and Wray worked closely with Don to continue to grow the company.

The competition among meatpacking companies was fierce, and Don was looking for ways to increase profits and maintain an edge over the competition. Only so much profit could be made from raw chicken, and Tyson had maximized profits by creating its own feed and engineering birds to fatten as quickly as possible. Don had a "grow or die" mentality and knew selling packaged foods would lead to significantly better profit margins. He also focused aggressively on acquiring other meatpacking companies to take over a larger market share each year. Tollett defined Don (and men like him) as "a business cowboy that just takes the shots."

With less than three million people, Arkansas is a state where the Tyson and Walton families have shaped politics and policies in the state and nation. Despite the profits made by Tyson Foods and Walmart, which are both based in Arkansas, the state routinely ranks among the most impoverished states with high infant and maternal mortality rates.

Although wealthy families exert an outsized influence on politics across the US, the conditions in Arkansas, including its widespread poverty, mean that Tyson has a stranglehold on the state. Tyson Foods and Walmart are revered and feared, and their family foundations fund universities, nongovernmental organizations (NGOs), and schools. Local media outlets often publish business-friendly articles about the two companies, and national media outlets mostly ignore Arkansas. Without scrutiny, Tyson Foods and Walmart hold almost absolute power and seem untouchable in the state. The profits from the companies, wealth created by primarily immigrant workers, fund state and national policies aimed at deregulation, policies that put the health and safety of principally immigrant workers at risk.

In the 1970s, Don Tyson met Bill Clinton, who was teaching at the University of Arkansas School of Law in Fayetteville. Although people say they shared an interest in local Democratic politics, they were both known for, as the language of that time described and celebrated, enjoying the company of young women. Don's public-facing image was that of a man with a Cheshire cat grin dressed in a khaki Tyson uniform with his name embroidered on the breast. Coverage of Don Tyson in the early 2000s described him traveling with a group of young women who attended his meetings with Wall Street analysts. Privately, he collected cars, spent time on his deep-sea fishing yacht, and visited Tyson company homes in England and Cabo San Lucas, Mexico. Don and Bill would form a mutually beneficial relationship, a political and financial quid pro quo that would last for decades. Don said of Bill's political acumen, "He was young and he was impressive." Though the two framed it as a friendship, their dealings would impact state and national meatpacking industry regulations.

Bill Met Don in 1974 and they remained friends until Don's death in 2011. Bill oversaw weakened environmental regulations that contributed to Tyson's growth. Bill rode around with Don in his Bentley and private plane. Tyson received nearly $8 million in state tax breaks for plant expansions under then-governor Clinton. Clinton's close relationship with the Tyson family and Tyson Foods would propel him to the White House. When Don Tyson died in 2011, many compared him to Arkansas natives Bill Clinton and Sam Walton, the founder of Walmart.

People often marvel that Bill Clinton, a Democrat, became governor of Arkansas, a conservative state that routinely votes Republicans into power. But Bill Clinton, as his predecessors had been, was pro-business. Arkansas is small and insulated. Much of the history surrounding Bill and Hillary Clinton and the Tyson family shows how the political and financial elite blurred the lines between friendship and financial dealings.

In 1978, Hillary Rodham Clinton met lawyer James Blair, the outside counsel to Tyson Foods. Blair advised Rodham Clinton to invest $1,000 in trades of cattle futures contracts, which generated nearly $100,000 in ten months. The deal was regarded as a possible conflict of interest and an attempt to gain influence with Bill Clinton, who was elected governor of Arkansas in 1978.

In the 1970s, when more women were entering the workforce, and fast-food empires were growing, Don saw an opportunity to sell packaged chicken products. Under his watch, Tyson Foods invented McDonald's Chicken McNuggets and the Burger King chicken sandwich, among thousands of other prepared food items. At that time, chicken was unpopular, so the company had to convince restaurant chains that it could be packaged as a healthier option than hamburgers.

In 1979, McDonald's, whose sales had dropped as consumers became more health conscious, contracted Tyson to make the chicken nugget. Tyson developed a custom breed of chicken with more breast meat for the nugget. McDonald's launched the McNugget in select markets in 1981 and at all franchises in 1983. As one of the first advertisements described, "A McNugget is a boneless chunk of tender, tasty chicken with four kinds of sauces to choose especially for dipping." In one close-up, a pair of disembodied hands break open a nugget, and steam rises from the white meat. Children and adults of all ages look in awe at the nugget and dip it into different sauces with delight as voices sing, "'Cause you deserve a break today with chicken cooked the McDonald's way." McNuggets became an instant bestseller. Tyson's prepared foods sold for much more than raw chicken and ushered in the golden era of fast food. Tollett and Wray were part of the team that helped develop chicken products in the 1970s and 1980s and oversaw explosive growth. Wray said of Don Tyson, "Mr. Tyson was a father figure for me."

Wray, who wore glasses and often broke into a lopsided grin, was folksy in a way that often invited comparisons to his friend Bill Clinton. As he built the company, his strategy for the corporate side of Tyson was to hire friends who, as it happened, trended very White. By 1995, the company had no Black people or women senior executives among its fifty-five thousand employees. Wray also preferred Christians. He said, "Well, I don't want to sound antiquated, but I still think that the things that I would look for, and I always have as I've interviewed people: What was their home life like? Did they grow up in broken homes? Did they grow up in a home where they had loving parents? How do you answer those questions legally anymore? I don't know, to hell with that." To assess religious values, he asked potential employees, "Did you grow up in the church?"

When asked to give an example of a leader he admired, Wray said Martin Luther King Jr. Wray described King as "Huge on leadership style. Had a vision. Knew what it was. Started with nothing. Had a vision, knew what it was. Gathered people around him. Sold that vision. Got people to buy into it. Communicated it. And look what he did. That's what makes leadership. He doesn't have to be the smartest." Wray explained that it was more important for a leader to gather people around than to be the smartest person in the room.

Tollett believed that Tyson's strength was its size as a dominant player in the meatpacking industry. However, he admitted that the company's scale made it more vulnerable: "I liken this company to an ocean liner. We're going down. And it takes a little time to turn. Our competition is in motorboats, and they are pretty quick. They can miss the ice. But if he's not very careful, I can run right over his ass."

As profits soared, Don crowned himself "Chicken King" and built a replica of the Oval Office at the Tyson headquarters in Springdale. At his office, the doorknobs have egg handles, the crown molding includes egg shapes, and a flock of hens is carved over the fireplace. When his father died in 1967, Tyson's revenue was $35 million; by the time Don left the business in 2001, it had grown to $7.4 billion.

Employees at the corporate Tyson offices were handsomely compensated. In the May 2000 internal Tyson interview, Tollett said he looked for corporate employees with "a burning desire to do better and get rich," adding, "There ain't nothing wrong with being rich." While corporate employees built mansions in sprawling gated communities in Springdale, line workers struggled to pay rent. Tollett framed the company strategy: "We learned to be relatively frugal while we were being very aggressive and growing the company." Line workers, who risked their lives to get Tyson's product to market, could barely make ends meet, while corporate employees and the Tyson family lived off the largess of the company's profits. While it is easy to be blinded by Tyson's wealth and the Tyson family story of a self-made man, there would be no profits without the workers.

Wray, aware that the lack of interpreters caused accidents, said in the same 2000 interview for internal company purposes, "We have got to do a better job of communicating in their language and not just being able to speak the language but communicate. They are two different things." He admitted that most accidents at Tyson plants occurred during late-night shifts when interpreters weren't available.

Tyson spent prodigiously on lobbying efforts and political donations in a bipartisan manner. Whether a Republican or a

Democrat was in charge, meatpacking regulations would remain lax for decades at the state and federal levels.

....

Bill Clinton served as Arkansas governor for two terms from 1979 to 1981 and 1983 to 1992—coinciding with record growth at Tyson Foods. Clinton fit well into the good old boy's network that ran the state, which involved measuring influence in terms of money, women, and private planes.

Clinton was governor when Tyson faced criticism from environmental groups for disposing of chicken litter in rivers and streams. Seen from an airplane, chicken litter looks like pyramids of dried waste. In huge volumes, animal waste represents a threat to waterways. When Clinton began his second term as governor in 1983, a sinkhole developed near a water treatment plant in Green Forest, and a million gallons a day of partially treated chicken waste from the Tyson plant drained into the underground water supply, which contaminated the local aquifer. After residents became ill, Clinton "declared 60 square miles of Green Forest an 'imminent health threat emergency.'"

As governor, Clinton placed Tyson executives on state boards that later made favorable decisions for the company on environmental issues. During his time as governor, Clinton gifted millions in tax breaks to Tyson Foods, eased environmental regulations in favor of the company, and spent $900,000 on road infrastructure in Pine Bluff when Tyson was considering building a $40 million processing plant in the city. Clinton and his wife traveled in Tyson Foods airplanes for free, and the company made campaign contributions and helped raise funds for his reelection campaigns and his candidacy for president.

In 1992, the year that Clinton ran for president, the annual revenue at Tyson was twice the budget of Arkansas. A big believer in the power of money to influence politics, Tyson has invested nearly $18 million in lobbying and $300,000 in campaign contributions per election cycle since 2010. Tyson Foods has contributed politically to Democratic and Republican presidents and focused on bipartisan lobbying efforts. Tyson backed both Clinton and Bush in their presidential campaigns. The company has significantly contributed to the lack of oversight in the industry for decades.

In 2005, the U.S. Securities and Exchange Commission (SEC) announced enforcement proceedings against Tyson Foods, Inc., and its former Chairman and CEO, Don Tyson. The SEC charged that from 1997 to 2003, Tyson Foods made misleading disclosures of perquisites and personal benefits provided to Don Tyson before and after his retirement as senior chairman in October 2001. For example, Tyson Foods paid Don $689,016 in cash advances to cover personal expenses for himself and two of his friends. These expenses included $20,000 for the purchase of Oriental rugs, $18,000 for antiques, $15,000 for a vacation in London, $8,000 for a horse, and other substantial purchases of clothing, jewelry, artwork, vacations, and theater tickets. The Tyson Art Collection includes 300 paintings, 151 sculptures, 149 prints, and 121 photographs, with works by Andy Warhol, Ansel Adams, and Robert Rauschenberg. Company profits, made at the cost of the health and safety of workers, were used by the Tyson family to fund a lavish lifestyle that included gifts to powerful politicians.

During his two presidential terms from 1993 to 2001, Bill Clinton and members of his administration maintained a close relationship with the Tyson company and the Tyson family. In 1994, however, the *Oklahoman* newspaper published a letter to the editor from Don Tyson titled "Tyson Grew Without Clinton." Don Tyson wanted to distance himself and the company from criticism that Tyson's growth was due to favorable treatment from Clinton. Tyson wrote, "As chairman of the board of the nation's largest and most successful poultry company, I am quickly growing weary of the insinuations and allegations that the company bearing my family name is in some insidious way benefiting as a result of the fact that the former governor of Arkansas now resides at 1600 Pennsylvania Avenue in Washington."

In 1997, Tyson Foods pleaded guilty to making $12,000 in illegal gifts to Mike Espy, the agriculture secretary during Bill Clinton's first term. Don Tyson and John Tyson, then the company's chairman and vice-chairman, respectively, were named as unindicted co-conspirators for their alleged role in arranging the gifts, which included football tickets, airline trips, meals, and scholarship money for Espy's girlfriend. The director of government and media relations at Tyson Foods, Archibald R. Schaffer III, was convicted of providing Espy with $2,500 worth of air transportation to attend a May 1993 Tyson family party in Arkansas. The company paid $6 million in fines and costs to settle accusations, and Schaffer and one other Tyson executive were convicted and received prison terms in the case. At that time, regulations affecting Tyson, including safe handling instructions on poultry packaging, were pending before the U.S. Department of Agriculture. The company argued that the gifts were an "act of common hospitality." President Clinton later pardoned the Tyson executives.

Tyson asserted control over the marketplace. In 1997, Tyson bought Hudson Foods for $642.4 million. Reflecting on that deal in the May 2020 interview, Tollett said, "In the case of Hudson, probably our most significant competitor in the marketplace, I think it was, in retrospect, absolutely the right thing to do to buy them."

Tollett argued that the company had the will to do things right but said, "We have been beat up the last three or four or five years about food safety issues, environmental issues ... We wore ourselves out talking about plant safety, workplace safety. Yet we get fined, and we have willful violations, which I think is ludicrous to me." Tollett complained, "And we had fines and have paid fines for willful violations in our workplace because some OSHA guy shows up and says here is a willful violation. That's wrong." He blamed labor organizations that "used" the Occupational Safety and Health Administration to create bad press about food safety issues.

To put Tollet's comments in perspective, OSHA has been understaffed for decades. In 2021, if OSHA needed to inspect all of the meatpacking facilities in the US, it would take them 165 years. And the average fine for a potentially life-threatening hazard that year was $3,700. It was cheaper to pay the occasional fine than to keep machinery, chemicals, and labor conditions safe for workers. Tyson Foods could control how injured workers were assessed and treated by opening on-site clinics. By treating most injuries with first aid treatments, regardless of severity, the company saved millions at the expense of workers' health.

Looking out at the woods surrounding his backyard as dusk fell, Víctor returned to his understanding of the story about Tyson leading the meatpacking industry. He said, "All the chicken companies are the same. When I was at the Tyson Berry Street Plant, there was a death. A guy was killed by a trailer. There was nothing in the news. Víctor heard that Tyson quickly settled the matter. "They have bought everyone," he said.

4

WHY DOESN'T GOD TAKE ME?

In the summer, Rosario got up before the sun rose and watered her celosia plants, an explosion of velveteen magenta-colored flowers, in her backyard in Rogers. Then, she made breakfast for her husband: eggs, tortillas, and beans. They ate breakfast together in the kitchen, sitting under a painting of the Last Supper, just like the one at Quetzali's house, surrounded by cactus plants.

After breakfast, she washed the dishes, gathered her things, took one last look in the bathroom mirror, and passed by a small, battery-powered watering can full of fake pink flowers that danced and played the tune "Walking on Sunshine."

On June 27, 2011, like every other workday, Rosario entered the plant on Berry Street with the other six hundred or so workers on the first shift. She gathered her protective gear and made her way to the debone line. Rosario worked on the packing line, surrounded by the other workers who were divided along fourteen different lines, where they deboned, washed, and cut chicken. Around nine a.m., out of the corner of her eye, Rosario noticed that workers on the other lines were suddenly slowing down.

Had she been able to look up, she would have seen a pale greenish-yellow gas gathering in the room. But she was focused on the chicken. Rosario felt burning, scorching in her throat, but when she opened her mouth, she couldn't breathe. It was like her throat was closed. Moments later, she saw employees run to the only exit, a partially closed door down a long hallway. But Rosario's line was still moving quickly, so she tried to keep up, confused. She covered her nose with her sweater, desperate for fresh air. Without even realizing it, she began to run to the door: "The chemical gas was concentrated in the hallway. But we had to go out that way."

The hallway leading to the exit seemed to Rosario like the distance between Arkansas and Mexico. Finally reaching the exit, she was blocked by supervisors who were yelling, "Don't leave! Everything is fine!" As they inhaled the gas, her co-workers started to faint around her, their bodies falling with a thud. Rosario said, "We wanted to run but couldn't, so we inhaled the chemical." She felt her mind separating from her body and thought she was dying. Then she slipped through the scrum—she wouldn't remember how—and woke up outside on the pavement, under the oppressive Arkansas sun. Martín Barroso lay nearby, and if Rosario had had the energy to look around, she would have seen his body there.

Springdale, a city of roughly seventy-two thousand people, had only four ambulances. While hundreds of workers lay on the pavement gasping for air, Tyson coordinated buses to take them to various local hospitals. Crammed in a bus, her lungs still hurting, Rosario rode from Springdale to a hospital in Rogers, which is only twenty minutes away but felt like years. She arrived at the hospital emergency room unconscious and was loaded onto a stretcher. She overheard a nurse speculate that she was DOA: dead on arrival.

In total, 173 workers were hospitalized that morning. But production at the plant continued. Workers on the second shift arrived, unaware of the accident. Plácido started the three p.m. shift and took his place on the cutting line.

One minute, Plácido was cutting chicken for patties, and the next, he felt like he was drowning. His nose and throat burned. He couldn't breathe and ran toward the nearest exit. Supervisors reprimanded him, but he continued to run. Once outside, a supervisor came to see him and allowed him to rest for an hour but then sent him back to work inside the plant.

Luckily, Angelina, who had been fired from Tyson, had found a job at another Arkansas-based poultry processing company and wasn't there that day. Tyson used a points system and once an employee accumulated fourteen points, they were automatically fired. For example, an employee who was absent the full shift without proper notification accumulated three points. Angelina had accumulated too many points.

It was easy to accumulate points. If workers didn't provide documentation for a list of approved reasons for "excused absences" at least thirty minutes before a shift, they were given points. During the first months of the pandemic in 2020, workers exhibiting COVID symptoms could not stay home and quarantine for fear of accumulating points—it wasn't an approved absence.

Tyson's point system gave the company a weapon that they could deploy against workers. Víctor described, "When Tyson has many people who have been there for at least fifteen years, those are the ones they want to fire the most. Because those people have a right to four weeks of paid vacation; they have more benefits than others. It isn't convenient for Tyson to pay someone for four weeks of vacation." When Tyson hired a new employee, that person received only one week of paid vacation and would have to wait ten years to reach four weeks. "Tell me: how much Tyson will save with the new worker?" asked Víctor. "They are saving a lot, which is the difference between a new worker and an old one. A person who has been there for years—if they make a small mistake, they get fired." But the worst part of what Víctor had witnessed was how the company humiliated workers. According to several workers, they are often asked to continue working before being escorted out by a security guard. Víctor asked, "Why does security have to accompany you? They humiliate you so that everyone will see you with security, and you will look dangerous. It is unbelievable; it is inhumane."

....

Víctor and Gloria worked different shifts and juggled childcare for their four children, who were all under sixteen. When Víctor had first been hired at Tyson, the company had provided information in Spanish—or whatever language the worker spoke, even Vietnamese. "Once you start work, however, there is no translator," he explained. "Every time there is an accident, they give us a document to sign where it explains the accident, but they don't provide it in our language."

By the time Víctor entered the plant at four p.m. on the day of the chemical leak, the fumes had mostly dissipated. According to several employees, Tyson didn't inform the second shift workers of the accident, Víctor had heard there had been an issue from co-workers. He wanted to investigate. "What exactly happened?"

he kept asking. His co-workers, many of whom had multiple family members who worked at the same plant, said that there had been an explosion.

At the time of the accident, the workers only knew they had been exposed to toxic chemicals, and not exactly what the chemicals were. At meatpacking plants, meat and poultry are refrigerated by using dry ice, which is often made from ammonia. An efficient and cheap refrigerant, ammonia is also toxic at certain levels of exposure. It can cause temporary blindness, eye damage, skin irritation, and severe lung injury. The chemical destroys respiratory passages and eyes by sucking water out of them rapidly. At high exposure, it can kill a person in seconds.

When mixed with chlorine, ammonia creates a toxic gas, chloramine, that can lead to coma and death. Germans first used the gas in warfare in 1915, killing over eleven hundred soldiers. The Geneva Protocol of 1925 prohibited chemical warfare with gasses, and chloramine has rarely been used since World War I. Ammonia and chlorine are commonly used at meatpacking plants to refrigerate and clean.

A December 2012 report on the incident at the Berry Street Plant in Springdale published by the Centers for Disease Control and Prevention (CDC) and entitled "Chlorine Gas Release Associated with Employee Language Barrier" stated: "On June 27, 2011, a worker at a poultry processing plant in Arkansas began to pour sodium hypochlorite into a 55-gallon drum that contained residual acidic antimicrobial solution. When the sodium hypochlorite reacted with the solution, greenish-yellow chlorine gas was released into the small room where the drum was located and then spread into the plant, where approximately 600 workers were present."

Víctor was a natural investigator and often wondered if he could be a journalist. In the weeks following the accident, he continued to talk to his co-workers. He described the desperation of those on the first shift to escape the chemical spill: "Everyone wanted to get out first, but they couldn't because the door was small. They piled up, and some fainted and fell like poisoned cockroaches." According to Víctor, "Some had been trampled, others had fractures; some pregnant women worried about losing their babies—thank God, they didn't. Many had burns—those close to the explosion."

Tyson publicly referred to the incident as a "chlorine gas leak" and reported that all 173 hospitalized workers returned to the plant within a few days without issue. However, the CDC's report noted that "Chlorine is a respiratory irritant and can produce symptoms ranging from mild eye, nose, and throat irritation to severe inflammation of the lung, which can lead to death. Of the approximately 600 workers who were evacuated, 545 were later interviewed and 195 reported seeking medical treatment, 152 reported being hospitalized, and the plant nurse reported that five were admitted to intensive-care units."

....

The chlorine gas release at the plant on Berry Street was just one disaster of many recorded. Between 2012 and 2021, Tyson plants in the US experienced nearly fifty ammonia leaks, injuring 150 workers—at least, those are the ones Tyson has acknowledged. Federal labor safety inspectors have noted poor maintenance and safety training at some plants where workers were exposed to known leaks and have investigated the company numerous times. It's been estimated that Tyson accounted for nearly six in ten ammonia-related injuries reported by meat processing facilities to the EPA.

Tyson has about one hundred facilities nationwide where enough ammonia is used to require reporting to the EPA. Combined, those plants have more than ten million pounds of the dangerous chemical. That puts the onus on Tyson to protect employees with robust safety precautions and training to prevent leaks like the one that hospitalized so many. In Springdale that day in 2011, workers said Tyson failed to protect them and then tried to cover up the cause of the leak.

In 2013, the Department of Justice sued Tyson following a spate of ammonia leaks, including one that proved fatal. The company entered a consent decree with the federal government, requiring Tyson to pay a fine representing a small share of the company's earnings and to review and, where necessary, repair pipes at some facilities. But the consent decree only included perhaps two dozen Tyson facilities—leaving out Arkansas plants.

After the chemical accident at the Berry Street Plant in Springdale, the company encouraged workers to return and the point system made workers feel they needed to return. On her first day back, Rosario fainted while deboning chicken. A co-worker brought her a wheelchair and took her to the on-site nurse at the plant.

Tyson offers on-site workplace clinics where occupational health nurses address worker injuries. Deborah Berkowitz, who served as chief of staff and then senior policy advisor for OSHA from 2009–2015, refers to workers in the meat and poultry industry as "captive patients" because if they seek outside medical care, they often face retaliation. The model is emblematic of others in the meatpacking and poultry industries, designed to

streamline efficiency, cut costs, and reduce liability, practices
that are being emulated by animal feeding operations further
down the supply chain.

"Oh, you're sick again?" the nurse asked Rosario with a
sigh. She dismissed the burning Rosario felt in her lungs. Rosario wondered: had she invented an illness? To live in a body
ravaged by the chemical accident was difficult, but to be made
to disbelieve oneself was worse.

Rosario has a recurring nightmare. She sees the greenish-
yellow toxic gas, and she can't breathe. But the line is still moving,
so Rosario knows she can't leave. Her vision dims. She sees only
pink as the chicken carcasses move down the line, each calling
for her knife as her lungs heave. She keeps her eyes on the line,
but her eyes burn, and she feels like she is suffocating. Like she is
drowning. When Rosario wakes up, she thanks God she survived.

. . . .

Plácido was hospitalized after the leak, struggling to breathe
independently. After the hospital discharged him, Tyson required
him to return to work immediately, just like Rosario.

"Look," Plácido told managers, "I'm screwed because of the
poison that was inside this plant."

They laughed.

Víctor, who was friends with Plácido, said of Tyson, "They
didn't do anything for him or others. The company should
have said, 'This happened. We should be more careful. If you
see something, notify us.'"

But in the days after the accident, Víctor didn't hear of a
meeting to discuss what happened or how to prevent it from

happening again. The Centers for Disease Control and Prevention released a report stating that the chlorine gas leak was caused by a worker who couldn't read the English-language label on a barrel of chemicals and inadvertently poured bleach into it. Tyson disputed the report, saying the federal investigators did not correctly identify the worker who caused the accident, a worker whom a Tyson spokesperson said was a native English speaker. As he asked around the plant for information, Víctor soon discovered Tyson's position. The company blamed an English-speaking supervisor who was alleged to have mishandled the chemicals.

"How is it possible they blamed one person when the company is to blame?" Víctor wondered. "The person needed training to know which chemicals he could mix."

Víctor said that the chemical accident didn't affect him because he was young and strong and because he was on the second shift, hours after the leak occurred, and in a different department. "But emotionally, yes, I was afraid," he added. He worried about how Tyson handled ammonia because ammonia pipes were everywhere in the plant. "The ammonia pipes pass above people. At any moment, they could explode. It could have happened here in the debone department at any time on any day," he said. He felt lucky that Gloria, who had been at work the day of the chemical accident, was stationed in a department far from the spill site and hadn't been affected.

Federal authorities would agree that more chemical training was needed. However, there was a key difference in the investigative report released in 2012 and Tyson's position. The report stated that Tyson had failed to provide a Spanish-speaking worker, who was expected to handle the potentially deadly chemicals with instructions in Spanish. Tyson spokesman Worth Sparkman denied that the worker responsible for the chemical accident was Hispanic. Sparkman presented an alternative narrative that an English-speaking worker who had been adequately trained in the use of hazardous chemicals simply made a mistake. The company strategy for dealing with the aftermath of accidents was to argue that there was no systemic problem, and that accidents were simply caused by individual workers.

Víctor wanted to expose the company's labor conditions. But how could he without risking his livelihood? "They have a policy that says we, as Tyson employees, can't speak to the media, whether it be the radio, a TV station, or a reporter," Víctor said. "According to their ethics, we must tell Tyson about any problem, doubt, or complaint. We have no rights. It is how they intimidate us. That is why people don't say or do anything—we fear losing our jobs."

Víctor explained that Tyson was good at hiding things. He described the managers and supervisors as being, "Mostly White," and how they used "dirty politics" to silence workers. Víctor explained, "When everything goes well at work, they never thank us because everything went well. But if something goes wrong, they ask us what happened." One day, Víctor was at work when a tool fell into the grinder and broke the blades that mixed the chicken nuggets. His supervisor replaced the blades. But two hours later, the supervisor returned with a legal document in English, which he asked all the workers in the chicken nugget area to sign. Víctor said, "They never gave it to us in Spanish. I don't understand why they have us sign things in English." Víctor understood basic English and read that there would be disciplinary action if a similar accident occurred again. "A disciplinary action is a verbal warning first, a written warning second, and getting fired third," he explained.

After the chemical accident, Rosario was left with a severe reaction to household chemicals, from Clorox to laundry detergent. Her big dream had been to become a beautician and open a salon. That, however, required working with chemicals. "Tyson ruined my dreams," Rosario said.

Plácido also became depressed. He had a persistent cough and couldn't sleep. "I can't endure it," he often said in the middle of the night. Angelina got up, gave him warm water, and rubbed Vicks and alcohol on his back and chest. The doctor approved by the on-site nurse at the clinic at Tyson had said Plácido was fine. But Plácido felt that his back would split open from pain. He felt useless even as he kept working. He asked Angelina, "Why doesn't God take me?"

5

MORE DEAD THAN ALIVE

One evening, Angelina stood in the kitchen, tying an apron around her waist, and said of Tyson firing her, "After they ran me off, I said, 'Thank God,' because possibly I would be sick like my husband."

Angelina said that Plácido, who had trouble breathing daily, was "more dead than alive." As he got sicker by the year, it seemed less likely they would return to El Salvador. Angelina said, "We said let's save some money and go. Since we arrived here, we haven't gone. We only have a work permit."

Plácido regularly visited the on-site Tyson nurses at work, complaining of shortness of breath and tiredness. They gave him Tylenol and sent him back to work. Eventually, he got approval from the on-site nurse at Tyson to visit a doctor. Tyson workers often spoke of "Tyson doctors" or "Tyson-approved doctors," because they could only visit a doctor once an on-site nurse had approved the visit and selected the doctor. Tyson runs on-site clinics via third-party providers like Marathon Health.

Angelina said of Plácido, "He used his vacation days to go to the doctor. He never had a week of vacation. Poor thing. I feel sad seeing him suffer. What can one do?" The difference between how he felt and how the nurses treated him made him question himself and break into tears at unexpected moments.

Every morning, Angelina made Plácido coffee. After the chemical accident, he had a hard time breathing in the morning and would ask her to rub Vicks on his chest instead. Angelina said that since that fateful day in June, "he began to have a persistent cough. He asked why he had a cough. He went to the doctor repeatedly with Tyson's insurance. The doctor never told him what was wrong."

In the months after the accident, Rosario also felt like "I hadn't recovered yet. I was weak. But Tyson wanted us to work." Even making breakfast in the morning felt beyond her, her breathing short and raspy, as if she had run a mile. Rosario said, "God has helped me recover spiritually. He allowed me to live, and I am profoundly thankful. Who was going to help me get out? Not Tyson, my God, my body and mind were gone, and I couldn't breathe. I arrived at the hospital with tachycardia and was about to die." She wondered why Tyson's supervisors hadn't warned workers about the chemical leak or tried to help them evacuate the plant as the leak was underway.

At Tyson, Rosario visited the on-site nurses regularly. She said of Tyson, "They never recognized what they did. They sent us to their own doctors who laughed at us. The doctors and the nurses did that, and it was devastating. They told me I was fine and had me return to work. I couldn't because I felt like I was going to die."

The on-site nurses assured Martín, Rosario, and Plácido that the chemical accident had not had a lasting effect on their health.

Even as their bodies told them they were in trouble, the on-site nurses repeatedly told them they were fine. Rosario said that, in truth, the chemical accident damaged workers "physically, psychologically, and financially. Supposedly, [Tyson's] doctor would cure us, but he didn't."

....

In 2014, three years after the incident and still desperate for help, Rosario visited the Northwest Arkansas Workers Justice Center, where she met Magaly Licolli. Short with dark hair and eyes, Magaly can command with a look, and was able to put people in their place without speaking. The Center aims to support religious congregations, workers, and community groups working to improve labor conditions. When Magaly began organizing, she didn't know much about labor law, but she wanted to support immigrant meatpacking workers in their fight for rights. She believed that change happens when you build power within people.

When Magaly graduated from the University of Arkansas in 2013 with a theater degree, she was disillusioned by the racism she experienced in the program. While she believed theater was a way to inhabit a role and free yourself from stereotypes, her experience at university had proved the opposite. After graduation, she began to work at the Northwest Arkansas Workers Justice Center in nearby Springdale, using her Spanish to help immigrants. She said, "I had to make a living, so I began working at the community clinic helping immigrants. Most of them were poultry workers or former poultry workers who were disabled due to injuries they suffered at these processing plants. I worked there for two years, and I saw a lot of desperation in my community that was suffering so much." Magaly witnessed poultry processing workers who had been injured for life and had no recourse for getting medical help or disability benefits.

As Magaly worked her way up to executive director of the Northwest Arkansas Workers Justice Center, she became frustrated with the model of the organization, which she felt didn't provide workers with the skills to change their industry. She said, "We needed to focus on empowering the people directly affected."

Rosario told Magaly that she had trouble breathing when washing dishes and couldn't be around household chemicals like laundry soap, so her husband had begun doing the laundry. While Tyson was supposed to regulate chemicals, Rosario found they were everywhere at work. She said, "Chemical use is out of control," noting that when she complained to the plant managers about the situation, "they get mad and annoyed."

Frustrated with what they perceived as Tyson's lack of action since the chemical accident—both in terms of dealing with the workers' health consequences and improving safety—Magaly and Rosario began to talk about organizing with other women working in poultry processing in Arkansas. However, Rosario said of her employer, "They don't want everyone getting together because they know two heads are better than one. When several of us meet, we think of ways to improve labor rights. We don't want to damage the plant; we want the company to care about justice. They can make a profit and we can have justice."

The Center was oriented to providing services rather than organizing workers, and Magaly became frustrated with that model. Locals in Springdale told Magaly and the poultry workers that nobody could challenge Tyson, creating a sense of powerlessness.

Magaly began to dream of starting an organization to support workers.

Magaly had listened to disabled workers, to those missing fingers and limbs. She said, "It was odd that nobody wanted to discuss it, to address those issues. Workers were living in the shadows. I was frustrated with the stories I heard every day. I asked myself, what can we do to change the situation?" Magaly often thought of the women who came into the clinic who had worked in poultry processing for so many years that their hands, sacrificed to repetitive motion, were no longer their own—some of them couldn't pick up a child or cradle a baby.

A feminist, Magaly wanted to organize workers and use theater to teach them about labor rights. As she met more Tyson workers who had survived the 2011 chemical accident, she wondered how to support them effectively. She knew how difficult it was for workers to share stories about labor conditions: "For them to speak to the media means they will be exposed. Companies like Tyson have mechanisms to retaliate against workers, to shut them down, and to fire them."

....

Like many citizens, Magaly didn't know much about Tyson's onsite nursing system. It was difficult to hear workers' stories and imagine a scenario where nurses did not help workers understand their medical condition or get necessary, even urgent, care.

One nurse who worked at the Berry Street Plant in Springdale and several other Tyson plants around Arkansas started working at Tyson after the chemical accident. She did not know Rosario or Plácido or their specific cases. Jenny, not her real name, said she did her best to treat workers, who she called "team members" per Tyson rules. The company protocol for musculoskeletal injuries allows nurses to provide ice and pain relievers for up to twenty-eight days, according to the employee manual, and the process can repeat if a nurse deems an injury unresolved along the way. That means Tyson's on-site nurses had twenty-eight days to treat workers with first aid: ice, rest, and ibuprofen. If nurses treated workers with first aid, Tyson was not required to report the injury to OSHA. Jenny admitted she had witnessed Tyson managers tell "a nurse not to document an injury."

Describing the on-site nurses at the Berry Street Plant, Mateo, a supervisor, said, "Nobody does anything if someone complains that their hands hurt. You go to the nurse's office, and they tell you to use two quarters to buy a pill for your pain." As a supervisor, he witnessed injured workers visit the on-site clinic, where they were almost universally told to buy pain medication from a small vending machine. "In my opinion, this is a clear example of when a nurse is not a nurse," he said, referring to the on-site Tyson clinic as a "black hole" of problems.

Once a year, the nurses gave hearing exams to workers. Mateo, who believed he had lost his hearing due to the noise at the plant, said the nurses gamed the system to help him pass the hearing test. On the day of the test, he said, "They gave me an early appointment so there was no noise at the plant. I took the test, and they shouted and congratulated me when I passed it. But I can't hear, so it doesn't mean anything if they say I passed the test. I can't hear anymore." And then he sighed and asked, "If they do that with me, what do they do to people who are injured?" Mateo described the nurses as "despotic" and said, "If you want to get anything from them, you have to fight for it." Mateo asked a manager why the nurses didn't send him to a doctor for a hearing aid. According to Mateo, the manager responded, "They only need more bodies in the plant."

Tyson's on-site occupational health nursing model is emblematic of others in the meatpacking and poultry industries, designed to streamline efficiency, cut costs, and reduce liability—practices that are being emulated by animal feeding operations further up the supply chain. The model reduces hospital trips and doctor visits that would otherwise trigger mandatory reporting to OSHA. The on-site first aid model at Tyson is standard across the meatpacking and poultry industry.

This model makes it hard to maintain federal oversight of injuries and opportunities for workers to receive paid time off, workers' compensation, and damages when they are hurt. Tyson has a history of lobbying to retool workers' compensation laws to benefit the company's bottom line. For workers like Plácido, Rosario, and Martín, the on-site nursing model allowed Tyson to delay and deny care. Rosario wanted to look for a different job but realized, "I can't do anything because I always cough. Even when I walk, it is hard for me to breathe. Even talking makes me tired." She added this about Tyson: "They harm you in every way. They don't care."

Deborah Berkowitz, who served as chief of staff and then senior policy advisor for OSHA from 2009-2015, explained, "Workers are sort of captive in these first aid stations because companies have policies that state that workers could be fired or disciplined if they seek medical treatment outside the company. Further, the companies make clear that they won't pay for any medical treatment unless the company sends workers to a doctor. OSHA found repeatedly that meat and poultry companies delay sending workers to a doctor for care, and OSHA found this led to worker injuries worsening over time. Most of these workers have no health insurance."

Workplaces are required to report severe injuries, including amputations, the loss of an eye, and others that require at least a one-night stay in a hospital, directly to OSHA within twenty-four hours. However, injuries that require a simple doctor's visit are recorded in company logs that feed into reports to OSHA annually. The agency uses those reports to plan inspections of high-hazard workplaces and direct its enforcement. The system is designed to efficiently use the limited number of OSHA inspectors. But companies can deflect OSHA's attention if the nurses they employ give injured workers first aid treatment instead of recommending medical care.

This is one of several reasons workers in the Tyson system are not allowed to consult with doctors about an injury unless the on-site nurse recommends it, according to a nurse and several plant workers employed by Tyson. If a worker wants to consult with an outside doctor, they are required to pay for their own care, which is what Plácido, Rosario, and Martín eventually were forced to do.

Víctor remembered the time chicken blood dripped into one of his co-worker's eyes. When the man's eye became inflamed, he went to an on-site Tyson nurse. He wanted to go to the hospital because his eye was painfully swollen, but the nurse said, "No, I'm going to help you here." The worker protested, "My eye is infected, and I could lose it." He was terrified when the nurse did nothing except give him Tylenol, so he asked Víctor for advice. Víctor told his friend, "If you lose your eye, you won't see the same. You need your sight to work." He said of Tyson, "They don't care. I have seen dead bodies at work, and they don't care." Víctor advised the worker to secretly pay for an outside medical consultation, which the worker did. The worker thanked Víctor for saving his eye.

....

At some point during her time at Tyson, Margarita began to go to the clinic to visit the nurses twice a day. "They gave me ice and told me to return to work. At night, I took medicine, but, oh, God."

By 2020, Margarita said, "They told me, yes, they were going to operate, but I had to threaten them." The doctor completed the carpal tunnel surgery on a Friday, and she was back at work by Monday. "They sent me back to the line, but I couldn't endure the pain in my hand."

Hearing of Margarita's situation, Berkowitz explained that in addition to documenting injuries, "OSHA regulations require companies to record how many days of work somebody misses due to a work-related injury. And so, this way, Tyson can say, 'I don't have any lost workday injuries.' This is all about public relations for Tyson—to attempt to hide the number and seriousness of injuries due to unsafe conditions."

Nurse Jenny said of Margarita's swift return to work after surgery: "That's very common to have someone have surgery and come back the very next day," adding that Tyson would lose "safe man hours" otherwise, which is the time a plant's workers have clocked without injury, also reported to OSHA. Medical experts typically recommend four to six weeks of recovery from carpal tunnel surgery, sometimes more. The Tyson-approved surgeon recommended one week of recovery, but Margarita's supervisor at Tyson told her that it was "not necessary to rest."

Tyson paid for physical therapy, but when Margarita finished it, she was sent back to the chicken wing line to do the same repetitive movements.

Derek Burleson, director of public relations at Tyson, in response to allegations that Tyson delays care for injured workers and does not provide proper time off to heal from surgery, wrote via email: "If a team member is injured at work and asks to see a doctor, our nurses are instructed to set up a worker's compensation claim. We pay for worker's compensation approved medical treatment, including consulting with outside doctors, and team members are not required to pay for their own care." Burleson said that Tyson employs "more than 1,100 health and safety experts in occupational safety, industrial hygiene, ergonomics, process safety, loss prevention, transportation safety, and other specialists who serve in key health and safety roles at our corporate and plant levels in support of the company's commitment to providing a safe and healthy workplace."

Standing in her living room, Margarita said of some on-site nurses at Tyson, "Supposedly, they are here to help you, but I don't think it works well because they don't help you—they only give you a little ice, and that's it, and then back to work." Jenny confirmed that these experiences were typical.

Alexia Kulwiec, associate professor of law at the University of Wisconsin-Madison, teaches labor and employment law and is an expert in national labor policy and workers' compensation. She said of the on-site health clinics at Tyson: "Their whole goal is not to find serious health problems and to keep costs down. It is really circumventing the whole purpose of worker's compensation to start with."

Margarita did not remember the nurses' names, noting that they changed frequently because it was a high-pressure work environment. She shared one experience in which a nurse told her that nothing was wrong and she was fine. Returning to the chicken wing line, Margarita was in so much pain she couldn't work. Another time, when she asked to see a nurse, her supervisor sent her to fill out paperwork. She said, "They send it to I don't know who, and they decide if you qualify to see the doctor." Margarita said she faced many challenges during the eight months she requested to see a doctor, adding, "I have to be dying."

Burleson, however, said via email that Tyson offers its workers a variety of avenues to address concerns about its processes, and that the company's employment policies encourage workers to bring such matters to the attention of management, human resources, Tyson's Department of Ethics & Compliance, or a confidential Tell Tyson First Helpline. "Complaints received through these avenues are investigated and worked to resolution," he wrote in the email, adding that workers are trained on these policies.

....

Nurse Jenny said that managers and supervisors at the Tyson plants where she worked often entered the room where she assessed patients and weighed in on a course of action. She confessed, "I don't know of any supervisors with a medical background." She spoke slowly, choosing words and pausing before finishing a sentence: "I think sometimes nurses aren't left to do their job properly, I believe, because people come in that are nonmedical, and they want to know what happened, what's going on."

Jenny commented that Tyson's management team had yearly goals to keep OSHA recordable injuries—any work-related injury or illness requiring medical treatment beyond first aid—below a certain percentage. She said, "If you were to take twenty nurse managers and ask them if they ever had pressure from their management, the answer would almost always be 'yes.'" Magaly explained that this system created "paranoia among the workers." Further, Berkowitz said of Tyson, "They could set the standard for what every other meat and poultry plant needs to do in terms of protecting workers on the job. And instead, they drive the standard into the ground."

Nurse Jenny's claims about delayed care at Tyson also appear in documentation from several OSHA inspections at meat and poultry plants and an investigation of the industry by the U.S. Government Accountability Office (GAO) that all found similar patterns. Rebecca Reindel, the director of occupational safety and health for the AFL-CIO, explained that the emergency medical technicians and licensed practical nurses at poultry and meat-packing companies "are focused on, one, getting people back to work and, two, not having it be reported."

Jenny said, "There can be a lot of pushback from upper management about taking someone to the doctor." Part of that included nurses being pressured to investigate whether employee injuries were preexisting. And since OSHA is understaffed, they can't check in regularly to ensure OSHA guidelines—that advise companies like Tyson to rotate employees through line jobs to avoid musculoskeletal disorders—are actually followed. OSHA also urges employers to provide early medical treatment to prevent permanent physical damage, another directive that Jenny said was hard to enforce given the pressure from managers at Tyson to delay care to injured workers and poor oversight from OSHA.

"Workers in these meat plants have incredibly high rates of carpal tunnel syndrome, but the meat industry has figured out a way to hide these rates from the public," Berkowitz said. "OSHA regulations require that only work-related injuries that are serious enough to require medical treatment have to be recorded on official company injury and illness logs. What the industry perfected is a way to avoid having to record these injuries—like carpal tunnel syndrome—by essentially delaying or refusing to send workers or refer workers to see a doctor to get treatment when they are injured or ill from work."

In its investigations, OSHA found that plants delayed medical care for injured workers, issuing a citation in one case and hazard alert letters in four others in 2015 and 2016. In the letters, OSHA noted that one plant appeared to use its nursing station to prevent injuries from appearing on the plant's log, and another had prolonged treatment for workers without referring them to a doctor, including a worker who had made more than ninety visits to the nurse. OSHA also found that a number of workers were fired after reporting musculoskeletal disorders at the former plant, some on the same day they reported injuries.

Magaly pointed to Rosario and Plácido's situation as an example of the on-site healthcare issue. Magaly believed that the doctors approved by Tyson had lied to both workers about the impact of the chemical accident on their health.

....

During the first years after the chemical accident, Angelina and Plácido didn't have money to pay for a doctor who wasn't covered by Tyson. So, Angelina talked to her brujo because he helped her ward off illness and resolve problems. "The brujo, the work of the witch, is to speed things up, to speed them up and make sure they pay for what they did," Angelina said, hoping Tyson would be held accountable. The brujo lived in Siloam Springs, some twenty-three miles from Springdale. The brujo was, like her, from El Salvador. She did not reveal his name and said he didn't like people to know too much about how he worked. In El Salvador, a brujo might use everything from traditional medicine to rituals, incantations, and communication with those who had passed on to help others resolve problems.

The brujo did his work, sometimes sacrificing goats, and years passed. Angelina, sighing, said, "My husband was healthy when he began work there. Then his lungs were affected by the ammonia." Tearing up, she shared how he often said, "I can't take the pain." When he returned from work from the night shift, he would wake Angelina, telling her, "Get up, old lady, rub my back. I can't endure the pain."

Angelina said of Plácido's experience navigating the Tyson on-site medical system, "After five years of enduring that, they didn't diagnose him, he changed doctors." The new doctor told Plácido, "The ammonia ate your lungs. You don't have one lung, and the other will be finished soon. You are going to die drowning."

6

THE CHAPLAIN

By 2016, Magaly started to see more refugees at the Northwest Arkansas Workers Justice Center office, all of whom were employed in poultry processing. She organized regular meetings and events for poultry workers to learn more about labor organizing. Around town, she sometimes felt the heat of eyes on her, and, when she turned, she always saw the same face. She thought perhaps a man might be following her.

One day, a chaplain employed by Tyson came to see Magaly at her office—the same man she had seen around town. "He told me to stop," she said of her efforts to organize poultry workers. The chaplain offered to set up a meeting with the directors at Tyson, but she refused unless poultry processing workers could attend it with her. The chaplain said, "I've been on the line with the workers. I know what it is like. It's not a dangerous job." Magaly responded, "You are forgetting something very important. You are paid by the company to be the chaplain. You are White, you are a man, and they will never treat you the same way they treat the rest of the workers. You forget your privilege." Taking a deep breath, she added, "To come to me and tell me that the workers are lying—you should be ashamed of yourself." Before the chaplain left her office, he said, "I came here out of love."

In 2000, Tyson launched a chaplaincy program that funded over one hundred chaplains at meatpacking plants in twenty-five states. The company framed it as a program to create a "faith-friendly" workplace for employees of all religions. In listing its "Core Values," the company says it strives "to honor God and be respectful of each other, our customers, and other stakeholders." Víctor, who witnessed the first years of the chaplaincy program at the plant in Springdale, said of the evangelical chaplain the company had hired, "Supposedly he is for all religions," but complained that he discriminated against Catholic workers. Víctor, who was being required to work on Sundays, went to speak to the chaplain in January 2021.

Víctor told him, "I don't work Sundays because I'm Catholic. My religion prohibits me from working on Sundays." The chaplain told him, "You have permission to attend Mass. After that, you can return to work." Víctor replied, "You don't understand what I'm saying: I don't work Sundays. I dedicate Sundays to God. I don't just go to Mass, and then it's over—Sunday is for God." Víctor and his wife, Gloria, noting that the chaplains shared information from private conversations with workers with Tyson managers, began to refer to the chaplains as "spies."

Frustrated, Víctor asked for a letter from his priest to present to his supervisor at Tyson. The company, he told his priest, had asked him to work on Sundays, which interfered with his family attending church and studying the Bible. He told Juana, a supervisor, that the company should respect a person's religion. He asked her for Sunday off, giving her the letter from his church. Juana told him the letter didn't mean anything, suggesting he go to church early and arrive at the plant on time for the afternoon shift.

The Tyson supervisors continued to ask him to work Sundays. Víctor, who wanted proof of the hypocrisy he was experiencing from a company that said it respected the religious beliefs of workers, decided to record a conversation with his supervisor on August 20, 2020. A reporter who was doing a story on Tyson had once gifted him a pen-shaped recording device. Víctor figured the pen would be less noticeable than a cell phone. The supervisor didn't speak Spanish, so a translator was present. The supervisor asked Víctor for a copy of the letter from his priest, the same one he had given Juana months earlier.

The supervisor spoke to Víctor at length about religious petitions: "We try to help as much as possible, but we also have to make the plant run. Imagine if fifty people come and say, 'I can't work on Sunday.' We would have a problem. We try to evaluate each situation to resolve it so you can fulfill your religious obligations and we can keep the plant running. That is what we try to do." The supervisor began to question Víctor about his schedule on Sundays. Víctor mentioned that the many Adventists who worked at the plant always got Saturday off. His supervisor responded, "The Catholic faith. I am Catholic, too. My family has been Catholic their whole lives, and our faith doesn't require us to not work on Sunday."

Every Sunday, Víctor went to church and studied the Bible with his children, he explained. His supervisor said, "Each situation is a bit different. Each question is different. The question of religion is very specific with some people and some beliefs.

Each person has their faith, and it must be respected. That is why the question that is important to each person is different. That is it. It doesn't mean that one person is correct and I am wrong."

Víctor said it was a simple issue to resolve. His supervisor responded, "We don't want to work Sundays. Nobody likes it. We must do it. We hope we won't work Sundays anymore. Sometimes you have to do it."

Magaly said the chaplains are loyal to the company because that is where they get their paycheck. Nurse Jenny said workers sometimes talked to Tyson chaplains about their illnesses and injuries. Because the Tyson chaplains report to the human resource manager, workers like Víctor worried about personal information shared in confidence being reported to management. Magaly said on-site healthcare at Tyson is a way to "control the health of the workers because they are seen as machines."

....

In 2019, Magaly and sixteen immigrant women poultry workers, including Rosario, founded Venceremos, a worker-based organization whose mission is to ensure the human rights of poultry workers. Magaly began by teaching poultry processing workers about their rights. She used printmaking, papier-mâché, and puppet-making to help workers organize around issues like fair pay and workplace safety. She said, "I use theater and art—that is how I engage with and organize workers. Via popular education we all learn from each other, and I like that." Although she knew there was a lot of work to be done, her first goal was to create a safe space for workers to share their experiences and feel heard and powerful. Once she made that space, she believed workers would act to demand better labor conditions.

Later that year, Magaly traveled with Rosario and several other women who were helping her organize poultry workers to Florida where they met with the powerful Coalition of Immokalee Workers (CIW). The CIW has organized workers since 1993, and, like Venceremos, it began as a small group of workers meeting weekly. Over the years, they developed a worker-led model and used protests and media campaigns to pressure retailers to source food ethically and encourage consumers to support just labor conditions. In 2011, the CIW launched the Fair Food Program, an agreement with the Florida Tomato Growers Exchange that supports workers by maintaining a third-party monitoring body to investigate labor violations. The program benefits some thirty-five thousand laborers, primarily in Florida. Participating retailers pay a small premium to growers that is passed on to workers—an extra penny per pound of tomatoes that, if all major buyers were to participate, would nearly double farmworkers' wages.

Magaly believed that the CIW model could change the poultry industry in Arkansas. The CIW trained workers to teach other field workers about their labor rights. A worker-to-worker educational model is an essential tool for organizers in sectors like agriculture and poultry: workers need to be offered classes in their native language—often at the place they work, since that is where they spend most of their time—and with visual forms of learning since some are illiterate. "It's more like, let's have fun and learn together," Magaly said.

Magaly and the founding group of Venceremos, all women from Mexico and Central America, hoped to coordinate with workers from other countries. Arkansas is also home to fifteen thousand

Marshallese—the largest Marshallese community in the continental US—and 30 percent of Tyson's workforce in Springdale is Marshallese. Climate refugees, the Marshallese are close-knit, and most of them live in Northwest Arkansas near Tyson headquarters.

The Marshallese began migrating from the Marshall Islands—a collection of twenty-nine atolls and five islands—to the Ozarks in the 1980s. The Marshall Islands have faced rising sea levels of about .3 inches per year since 1993, which is twice the rate globally. The meatpacking industry in Arkansas began to recruit among the community, which faced limited employment opportunities and low wages in the Marshall Islands. As the concentration of Marshallese in Arkansas grew and word of the low cost of living spread, more and more people left the Marshall Islands for Arkansas.

Because the US tested sixty-seven nuclear bombs in the Republic of the Marshall Islands in the mid-twentieth century, the Marshallese were offered the opportunity to live in the United States under the Compact of Free Association in 1986. The Compact of Free Association allows them to travel back and forth between the Marshall Islands and the US and work in the US. However, because they aren't citizens, the Marshallese are not eligible for medical care and often have no health insurance. The Personal Responsibility and Work Opportunity Reconciliation Act of 1996 made the Marshallese ineligible to access federal Medicaid programs.

"As organizers, it will be a challenge to bring workers together," Magaly said. "All workers are affected by the company's policies and practices."

Magaly noted that, as Central and South American workers became more organized and demanded safer labor conditions,

Tyson partnered with refugee organizations to provide poultry processing jobs to refugees. It was a beneficial arrangement for Tyson because "at the end of the day, workers can't speak up because they fear losing their work permit."

Tyson often had a difficult time contracting workers. Tyson framed it as a labor shortage rather than discussing worker injuries and death rates, that the yearly turnover of workers was very high at some plants, or stagnant wages. The company found a solution by forming partnerships with refugee organizations in the early 2000s, recruiting workers with immigration papers. Between 2009 and 2021, an estimated 140,000 Karen, a large and dispersed ethnic group from Southeast Asia, have resettled in the US. Many worked at meatpacking companies like Tyson.

Refugees like the Karen make ideal meatpacking workers because, unlike Mexicans or Central Americans, they couldn't return home to visit family. Whereas Tyson workers from Mexico might take several weeks off at Christmas to see family in their home country, Karen refugees would continue working.

Refugees from Myanmar began to resettle in Arkansas around 2010. Ler and his wife, Haythi, from the Karen ethnic minority in Myanmar, met at a refugee camp in Thailand. The Karen, a primarily Christian minority, have suffered decades of violence at the hands of Myanmar's military.

Ler, a short, sinewy, silent sanitation worker, would start his shift at the Tyson plant in Clarksville, Arkansas, at midnight. He worked with water and chemicals, although he didn't know which ones. He didn't speak English, and while Tyson provided a Karen interpreter at times, he was often on his own. Each morning, he returned home to the two-room apartment he shared with Haythi and their four children. Ler entered, showered, went directly to the bedroom they all slept in, and fell asleep on a mattress on the bare concrete floor. Many Karen refugees who worked at Tyson lived in the same run-down apartment complex.

Haythi stayed at home with their four kids. She often wore a woven fuchsia ankle-length longyi, a traditional skirt, and walked around the house barefoot, her feet calloused and cracked around the heels. She wanted to work but was illiterate, didn't speak English, and didn't know how to drive. She didn't know her birth date, but she estimated that she was in her forties and her husband in his thirties. She talked about fleeing the military in Myanmar as they burned crops and killed Karen people. There was a constant food shortage at the refugee camp in Thailand where she spent six years.

She said matter-of-factly that living in Myanmar was harder than living in Arkansas because there she had to run to escape the military that tried to kill her people. Haythi said that compared to her home country, Arkansas presented no challenges. "I prefer to live here because I don't have to defend myself from the Burmese military," she said.

Prezena, also Karen, arrived in the US in 2012. Given the situation in Myanmar, the Karen were particularly afraid of doing anything that would upset Tyson or affect their status in the US. Prezena made $12.75/hour working six days a week in sanitation at the Tyson plant in Clarksville.

"What does that tell you?" Magaly asked. "[Tyson is] not even providing for people in the state. They are creating this kingdom to exploit people," she added. Of the immigrant workers, she wanted to make it clear: "It's not that they hate working—they love working. They are hardworking people."

Magaly believed Tyson hired immigrants and refugees because: "It creates the perfect environment for the company to keep workers divided. If workers don't understand the languages spoken by other workers, they won't understand the cultures or dynamics—they will be divided. And therefore, it is going to be difficult to unite workers and fight for better working conditions. The demographics in the plants benefit companies more than workers. It is well known that these corporations need vulnerable workers. The most vulnerable are the best workers."

. . . .

Elvira, a Mexican immigrant like Magaly, was one of the original sixteen women who helped found Venceremos. Elvira worked at Tyson's Chick-N-Quick Plant in Rogers for two years on a line pulling apart frozen chicken breasts so they could be cut and covered in breadcrumbs. When she started work in 2015, she said Tyson did not give her a single document in Spanish, her native language. Elvira said, "They have to treat people right. We all have rights, and we aren't robots. They treat us, the people, as if we were robots."

At work, she argued, "They need to provide us documents in Spanish. We are blindly signing things we don't understand." When she said that she knew her rights as a worker and should receive documents in her language, her supervisor began harassing her. He refused to let her go to the bathroom. Elvira told the many undocumented workers at the plant that they had the same rights as her and not to be afraid.

Elvira felt that the stress of the work situation led to partial body paralysis from a stroke. She spent over a month in the hospital and then went to rehabilitation. Although Tyson management mistreated her, she said the workers from Laos had it the worst—supervisors called them "Chinese."

After the stroke, Elvira sued Tyson to get them to cover the cost of her hospital bills. She said, "I support Venceremos because I want to resolve all the injustice." She found it surreal that Tyson didn't respect the most basic rights of workers, including bathroom breaks. She said of her supervisors, "They make a list, and you can't go to the bathroom if you aren't on the list." Elvira wanted everyone to know what was happening at Tyson. "I want justice," she said.

Venceremos belongs to the Food Chain Workers Alliance with over thirty other organizations that represent some 375,000 food-processing and agricultural workers in the US and Canada. Worker-based organizations are a powerful force for change because the people who most intimately understand the labor conditions give voice to the issues that must change to keep them safe. And there is power in numbers because workers can share strategies and teach each other about fundamental rights, which makes everyone feel less alone and terrified. But Magaly struggled to raise the funds she needed for translators and other staff to involve the refugees in Venceremos. When it came to dividing workers from different ethnic groups, Tyson had succeeded.

PART II

7

THE DISAPPEARANCES

I n the spring of 2020, around the time the water moccasins come out seeking warmth, the absences became undeniable. At meatpacking plants, managers and supervisors asked: where is this body or that body? Because they needed more bodies.

I often swam in the Little Mulberry River where water moccasins sunned themselves on rocks. The river runs along the edge of my parents' property in the Ozarks. With the arrival of COVID, I knew the choice the industry faced given my reporting experience in the meatpacking industry: follow the CDC's social distancing recommendations and decrease COVID infection rates thus decreasing production, or continue on as though COVID did not exist. Decreasing production would mean less profit, something I knew the industry would never stand for, no matter whose lives hung in the balance.

That spring, I applied for and received a grant from the National Geographic Society to interview meatpacking workers and publish an article about labor conditions during the pandemic. I rented a house down the road from my parents that had been built by my dad's twin brother. I knew that conducting interviews during COVID would be complicated, and I wanted to ensure that if I became infected, I would not put my parents at risk. There was no cell phone service and poor internet in the area, so I interviewed meatpacking workers via landline on a black rotary phone, sitting in a chair covered in orange velvet.

I reached out to Arkansas organizations that worked with immigrants and asked them if they knew any meatpacking workers who would be willing to speak to me anonymously. And that is how I learned that, despite the pandemic, many Tyson plants continued to process the maximum number of chickens per minute allowed, 140, even with fewer workers. Some plants had obtained permits in 2018 to increase the speed of the lines to 175 birds per minute, which continued during the pandemic. The more chickens processed, the closer the workers were to each other—and many of them worked in temperatures conducive to the spread of the virus.

As workers started to go missing, supervisors asked Gloria and others to pick up the slack, either by doing the work of two or three people or by managing machinery they hadn't been trained to operate. Gloria had seen the news about the arrival of coronavirus in the US, but nobody talked about it at work. In early 2020, standing in her kitchen while she formed the dough for pupusas, she said, "We realized a co-worker was infected because they disappeared. We asked Tyson, and they said not even one person was infected."

"Not even one," repeated Víctor. "The lines have half their capacity—many workers are missing," he noted, adding, "Lately, there have been a lot of accidents because when you're working more rapidly, you can't pay attention 100 percent to the dangers you are exposed to. You can fall because the floor is slippery, and you are running faster." The line where he made chicken nuggets operated at a maximum velocity of 250 revolutions per minute regardless of the number of workers. "I say revolutions because the machine that makes nuggets is a mold like the mold that makes tortillas that has the form of the tortilla and grabs a piece of dough. In only one turn, it makes fifteen lines of nuggets," Víctor said.

Who had COVID? Nobody knew. Workers tried to trace cases, with word of infections spreading through a whisper network.

Víctor said, "We realize when people are sick because we all know each other. I ask, 'Why isn't the guy at the machine here? I think he is infected.' And that's how we figure it out ourselves because we don't see them working. And they are gone for five days, and then they return. Even if they are infected, if they don't have symptoms, they can work almost immediately and only be at home for two or three days." According to workers, Tyson told workers who tested positive for COVID they could lose points if they stayed home from work.

It was in the early months of the pandemic that the reporter had interviewed Víctor and given him the audio recorder that looked like a pen. The reporter had asked him to wear it inside the plant and record conversations, which was against the law in Arkansas. Although it was against the rules, Víctor had previously kept a small cell phone in his pocket to document the quality of the chicken and the infestations of weevils, worms, and other insects around the plant. When he was offered the recorder, he agreed to use it and send the material to the reporter on the condition that he remain anonymous. But even after the reporter left Arkansas and published his article, which was critical of Tyson, Víctor kept recording conversations at work with the recording device that looked like a pen: "I began recording in the pandemic because I saw Tyson's injustices against all of us workers. I was willing to take the risk because I knew nobody would believe what was happening if it wasn't recorded." He wanted to document conversations that showed the company's willingness to lie and put workers at risk to keep production up during the pandemic. And he found meaning in those rebellious acts—he believed they would help hold the company accountable.

At the Berry Street Plant, new banners appeared: "We are feeding the country," and "If you have a complaint or a question, ask Tyson first."

....

At the beginning of 2020, Magaly was busy organizing Venceremos meetings with workers to discuss the high use of chemicals at poultry processing plants. She said, "We were going to begin addressing the concerns and to build on the campaign and the demands of workers. But then we had the pandemic, and we stopped having in-person meetings in late January." As workers began to hear about COVID, she remembered their worry. Many were already sick with respiratory problems caused by exposure to chemicals. "They immediately saw that they were high risk because of how close they were to each other, how they all get crammed in small halls at the plant," said Magaly.

Venceremos was less than a year old, and Magaly found herself alone in the pandemic: "We didn't have the necessary staff or money, but we did as much as we could." Magaly wanted to build trust with workers, to show them that it was possible to stand up against Tyson's labor practices. She explained, "For the first time, workers are willing to speak out against this company, and this is nothing we've seen before. Before, nobody said anything bad about them. We experience retaliation and isolation. This is the work, and it has to be this way until people understand what it takes to build something from the bottom up."

By March, Tyson had yet to provide workers at Rosario's plant in Springdale with masks. Instead, the company asked workers to make their own masks. Tyson instituted temperature checks for all workers, but Magaly said, "I always argued that it was not a real measure because there were asymptomatic people who didn't have a fever." At that point, workers had no options for paid sick leave. Instead, Tyson allowed them to request short-term disability, but workers reported that it was difficult to file claims because it was via a third-party company.

Rosario felt she would die if she didn't leave Tyson. Given her respiratory condition, if she got COVID, she would not survive. One day in early March, she woke up and could not get out of bed. The entire country was going into lockdown. On March 13, Tyson suspended all business travel and mandated that nonessential employees at its corporate office work remotely.

Magaly recalled, "I saw all these desperate workers. OSHA wasn't doing anything to enforce COVID protocols in meatpacking plants. Everything was just suggestions, guidelines, but there was no enforcement," she said. In the spring of 2020, OSHA implemented an emergency temporary standard for healthcare workers, but they didn't do the same for the meatpacking industry.

The workers who participated in Venceremos had immediate goals requiring Tyson plants to follow the CDC guidelines, including adequate personal protective equipment (PPE) and social distancing. "The companies had to decide to either protect workers or increase profits. It was black or white, and they decided to keep up with their profits and never cared for workers," said Magaly.

Further, Venceremos tried to tackle the lack of transparency at the meatpacking plants. "They were not notifying workers about exposures. They were not putting workers in quarantine," said Magaly.

....

The Arkansas Department of Health decided that if a workplace had less than five cases, the company didn't have to notify them. Tyson kept saying they had less than five cases. And the department of health did not require meatpacking plants to do contact tracing. "If they were going to do contact tracing, they would have to shut the company down," Magaly said of the Department of Health.

By May 2020, Tyson public relations officials were sending emails to the mayor of Springdale, telling him how to respond to questions about the rising number of COVID cases at meatpacking plants. Magaly said the leadership at Tyson was "very afraid. They wrote internal emails to elected officials to let them know that I was a radical union organizer. They were pretty much writing the speeches for these people. That Tyson writes the speeches for elected officials—it's bizarre."

In response to Tyson's attempt to control the narrative, Magaly supported workers who were afraid, providing them with options for sharing their stories, even anonymously. Magaly said, "We are in very isolated, rural, White communities where workers get punished for talking bad about Tyson. It is not that workers are afraid—there is no space or environment for workers to speak up." When journalists contacted Magaly, she tried to educate them about the threats workers faced to make the journalists understand that workers would need to be anonymous or use a pseudonym to protect themselves and their families. She said of workers, "A lot of them were afraid, and for them, I had to encourage them to speak to the media. And for them, sometimes it felt like a relief."

Gloria was quieter than Víctor, but she was the first to become interested in labor organizing. In 2019, she attended a Venceremos meeting, and Víctor became involved only at her insistence after COVID started. Magaly said women were at the forefront of the movement to create a safer workplace at Tyson. Gloria worried about getting COVID at work and passing it on to her children.

On May 28, 2020, a supervisor informed the workers on Gloria's line that eight or nine people had tested positive, but, as she recalled, "they said nothing was wrong and those people had been out of the plant for fourteen days and we shouldn't be afraid." That day, a Thursday, she took the COVID test at work and was asked to return to work the following day. But that didn't make sense to her, so she stayed home. She said it wasn't clear how the company treated COVID-positive workers: "They only gave workers who tested positive a week off, and then they called them and asked them to return to work. Those who didn't have symptoms were asked to return immediately. Workers went to human resources to ask why the company was asking employees to work with COVID."

"On April 7, we were all afraid," Gloria said. People in her department discovered that a co-worker had tested positive, but Tyson didn't inform the workers in the same area who could have been infected. Gloria said of her co-workers: "But then they began to leave and die, and Tyson never told us anything. When they didn't return, you realized the person had died. They don't tell you. A person in the department called the family to ask how our co-worker was. They said they had told the supervisor that he had died. But nobody told us."

"There is always a lack of workers," said Gloria. She noted that the policy Tyson communicated to workers was a "relaxed" attendance policy, and, in May of 2020, the company waived the waiting period for workers to qualify for short-term disability. Workers who tested positive for COVID and needed to quarantine could get 90 percent of their normal pay until the end of June. However, workers said the process for applying for short-term disability was complicated. Because lines were empty, they asked any workers who didn't have severe symptoms to return to work. Gloria's mother-in-law, who also worked at Tyson's Berry Street Plant, had tested positive for COVID. An on-site Tyson nurse from the Berry Street Plant called Gloria's mother-in-law while she was in quarantine and told her that if she didn't have severe symptoms, she needed to return to work.

Workers who tested positive for COVID and had to quarantine because they were symptomatic were supposed to be paid by Tyson during that time. But when Gloria talked to workers who had COVID and asked them whether they were being paid, they often said, "We didn't qualify." Tyson often structures payments via third-party systems that require, for example, workers with COVID to appear in person to fill out paperwork to receive their payments. Due to the nature of COVID and wanting to prevent the spread of the virus, many workers simply couldn't go to work to fill out the paperwork in person and, therefore, weren't paid while in quarantine.

Worried about the spread of infections among her co-workers, Gloria spoke to a woman in human resources. The woman, who spoke Spanish, told Gloria that COVID infections could spread because the Arkansas Department of Health permitted Tyson to let workers return without showing proof of a negative COVID test. Workers could easily still be infected. The woman gave Gloria advice, telling her to take two weeks off work and hope infection rates would be lower by the time she returned. But the woman was scared and whispered to Gloria that if Tyson management found out what she had advised, she would lose her job.

When she saw more and more co-workers disappear, Gloria decided to take two weeks off work as the HR woman advised, rather than risk getting COVID. At that time, Tyson was still punishing workers with points for missing days. Gloria said, "If I don't go tomorrow and don't call, they add three points. They are erased the next year on the same date. But if I call, they add one point. If I accumulate fourteen, I don't have a job anymore."

When she returned to work at the end of April, she did what she could to avoid her co-workers given the continued lack of COVID prevention. She ate lunch in her car and avoided the bathroom at lunchtime when it was crowded, making social distancing impossible. She said, "I am afraid because many are infected."

....

By April of 2020, COVID infections had spread across Arkansas like wildfire, which was later exacerbated by the state legislature lobbying against preventative measures like wearing masks. Venceremos workers developed new demands: to contain the virus, Tyson should shut down plants, deep clean them, and do contact tracing. Magaly found herself investigating which workers had COVID and how they might have gotten infected.

She said, "It was a lot of work that we were doing on tracing cases, tracing deaths, trying to get in contact with the families. Nobody was talking about these workers at all."

Víctor feared getting COVID, mainly because, like Gloria, he worried about infecting their four children. He confronted his supervisor, Bill, on April 10, 2020, with his concerns and recorded the conversation. Again, a translator was present because his supervisor did not speak Spanish. Calm and collected, Víctor began by saying, "Truthfully, I don't feel safe with coronavirus here."

He went on, "I am worried because I have four small children. It doesn't help them stay home from school if I could infect them due to my work." Bill told him not to worry because COVID didn't exist in Northwest Arkansas.

Besides, Bill continued, Víctor's work was essential: "Our overall mission right now, the reason why Chick-N-Quick is open and producing chicken is because it's going straight to the store to feed people. You go to the grocery store, and there's a lot of things that aren't on the shelves, and there's people that are looking for food. If we weren't running, if we weren't producing chicken, there would be a lot of hungry families out there right now. That's why you are doing the job that you do—the job that we all do here to keep us moving in the right direction and being as safe as possible is critical to the nation right now."

Bill asked Víctor, "What would happen if Chick-N-Quick closed tomorrow?"

Víctor repeated, "What would happen?"

Bill said, "We wouldn't have any food."

Víctor replied, "But we wouldn't die."

But Bill didn't stop there. He said, "Not every family has prepared the way that you have, Víctor. So, there's a lot of people that have to go to the grocery store today to buy something to be able to eat. But if we were to stop making chicken or Tyson as a whole quit making chicken, there would be families that would starve."

Still calm and composed, Víctor said, "I understand that perfectly."

Bill responded, "The illness is going to kill some, perhaps a million and a half people, but if Tyson stops producing chicken, hundreds of millions will die."

Managers and supervisors at Tyson were mainly White, like Bill, and mostly monolingual English speakers, like Bill. Even before the pandemic, Víctor recalled, managers and supervisors rarely spoke to workers. "I don't know why. I don't know if it is racism. I don't know if the company says they shouldn't speak so much to workers. The big managers are like that. I don't know why," he said.

. . . .

In the first weeks of April, the meat processing industry spent weeks lobbying the Trump administration. On April 26, 2020, John H. Tyson, the chairman of the board at Tyson Foods, published full-page ads in the *New York Times*, the *Washington Post*, and the *Arkansas Democrat-Gazette*. The founder's grandson made a similar argument to the one Bill had made to Víctor: "In small communities around the country, where we employ over 100,000 hard-working men and women, we're being forced to shutter our doors," he wrote in the ad. "This means one thing— the food supply chain is vulnerable." If Tyson had to close its facilities, which could save workers' lives, he argued that the nation would face a "limited supply of our products."

In the ad, Tyson did not mention that meatpacking plants were second only to prisons as the most significant sites of COVID infections in the US. As meatpacking workers were infected, became disabled, and died, companies like Tyson, Cargill, Smithfield Foods, and JBS continued to lobby the government to keep plants open. One day after John Tyson's ads were published on April 27, President Donald Trump issued an executive order declaring meatpacking plants "critical infrastructure" under the Defense Production Act of 1950. The order prohibited state health authorities from closing meatpacking facilities and provided legal cover from liability claims by employees disabled or killed by COVID. The order kept meatpacking facilities, which were virus hotspots, open, but it didn't impose federal rules requiring companies to protect workers from COVID outbreaks. On June 15, Governor Asa Hutchinson of Arkansas signed a limited liability executive order, which protected businesses like Tyson from liability related to COVID-19. The order would make it almost impossible for employees or their families to sue Tyson for wrongful death, for example, if a loved one died of COVID.

Lisa Pruitt, a University of California at Davis School of Law professor, said workers were unlikely to know about the liability shield or understand its import. Pruitt explained the order "comes into play when the plaintiffs [like workers who are sick with COVID or who have lost family members] start shopping around for an attorney, and it's just one more barrier an attorney is going to consider before taking a case—because it'll have to be taken on in court. Whether these liability shields are enforceable is one more legal unknown to be litigated."

Pruitt calls limited liability executive orders "constitutionally questionable" because the executive authority under which they have been issued, in the context of an emergency, is largely untested in the courts. "Certainly, they complicate any wrongful death lawsuit a worker's family might bring against a meat processor," she said.

On March 2, 2021, Gary Mickelson, the senior director of public relations at Tyson Foods, wrote in an email to me that workers were told not to come to work if they have the virus or were exposed to it and should return "only when they have met the criteria established by both the CDC and Tyson." He added that workers who tested positive were eligible for short-term disability pay, though as we've seen, sick workers needed to appear in person to fill out the paperwork. Mickelson did not respond directly to questions about limited liability shields. He listed the benefits Tyson had offered to workers during the pandemic, describing them as "including health and life insurance as well as short-term disability coverage. One hundred percent of our team members have health insurance, either through the company or another source, and the majority of the cost of the insurance we provide is covered by the company. We expanded our short-term disability coverage so those who get sick from the virus can continue to receive pay."

....

Sitting in the living room, his laptop computer on the edge of the TV stand, Víctor clicked on a video he had recorded on April 7, 2020. He told me, "You will see that when they take my temperature, the nurse isn't wearing a mask." He had recorded the video from his car as he entered Chick-N-Quick. In May, the company began to give workers masks, but Víctor worried because they weren't medical-grade masks, just cloth ones. "They say that those of us who have become infected, it is our fault because we became infected outside." When he asked his supervisor, Bill, why the company blamed workers for infections, he said, "You are getting together at parties and in big groups, and that is how you get infected." Looking up from the video he recorded clandestinely, Víctor said, "How dare they blame the workers? They say that if a person infected other people at work, that person got infected outside and brought it to work."

That same month, at a Tyson plant in Waterloo, Iowa, the plant manager of the facility, organized a cash buy-in, winner-take-all betting pool for supervisors and managers to wager how many employees would test positive for COVID-19. Like those in Arkansas, Tyson line workers in Waterloo reported that managers told them "they had a responsibility to keep working to ensure Americans don't go hungry." When news of the betting pool became public, the outcry led to an investigation. Court documents alleged company supervisors were instructed by the defendants to falsely deny the existence of "confirmed cases" or "positive tests" within the facility as early as March. These reports confirmed what Víctor and other Tyson workers in Arkansas had experienced. Gary Mickelson, the Senior Director of Public Relations at Tyson Foods, responding to questions about the Waterloo incident via email, said, "As noted in December by our president and CEO, 'The behaviors exhibited by these individuals do not represent the Tyson core values, which is why we took immediate and appropriate action to get to the truth. Now that the investigation has concluded, we are taking action based on the findings.'"

"There is no social distancing. It is impossible," said Víctor, noting that the only way to increase the distance among workers was to decrease production, which Tyson refused to do. He went on, "I know that I shouldn't be close to other workers. I try to be alone. My friends try to protect themselves because the company doesn't care. Some wear double masks. Some go and eat outside alone. I don't go to the lunchroom because it is very small. The company isn't doing anything. They have left us to our own devices.

"When they said, we are feeding the country, it was a lie because they were exporting chicken to China. I knew it because I saw it in the news," said Víctor. "They gave us this shirt, but we added some additional letters," he continued, showing me the shirt. It read, "Tyson, we feed the nation," to which Víctor had added the words "of China."

. . . .

In July of 2020, Tyson worker Randy, thirty, from the Marshall Islands, was still awaiting his COVID test results. Randy had been working at Tyson since 2018. The podcast "Arkansas Atoll," which covered the lives of Marshallese poultry processing workers during the pandemic, noted: "During the COVID-19 pandemic, the Marshall Islanders in the area have been disproportionately affected by the virus, accounting for half the deaths in the region."

When the Marshallese left the islands for Arkansas, their traditional diet of coconut, breadfruit, bananas, and rice changed, and their health suffered. The community is also afflicted with health issues related to radiation exposure on the Marshall Islands, as well as high rates of diabetes, obesity, and heart disease—risk factors that make them more susceptible to severe cases of COVID. Many of them work at Tyson to help pay for medical bills related to radiation exposure and other health issues. Like the households of many Hispanic workers, the Marshallese often live in multigenerational homes. During the pandemic, Marshallese workers at Tyson faced the added worry of infecting loved ones.

In early 2020, Randy became scared of contracting what he called "the sickness." With so many people at work, it was hard to be socially distant from anybody. When he went to work on June 8, 2020, he was flagged at the entrance because he had a high temperature. Tyson required him to get tested for COVID and stay home while he waited for the results. By July, he had yet to receive test results or be paid. Unable to pay rent, Randy, along with his wife and their two kids, received an eviction notice.

Randy asked his wife to call Tyson since she spoke better English than him, but he said Tyson didn't explain the situation. Some Marshallese speak only their native language, and workers like Randy often felt frustrated and confused given the lack of interpreters available at Tyson. The Marshallese community came together to help him pay rent, and, eventually, he found another job. Joena, a member of the Marshallese community and friend of Randy's, said, "I believe Tyson is taking advantage of the Marshallese community here since they have no clue of their rights here in America."

Víctor knew workers who got COVID and recovered and others who died. He knew a worker with a $35,000 bill from COVID treatment at the hospital. Víctor said, "The bill arrives, and who will pay it? Tyson won't pay it. If Tyson isn't paying for quarantine for workers, they aren't paying for you to stay in your house because you are afraid of getting infected."

Magaly said that, by June of 2020, "Lots of Marshallese were dying every week. And for poultry workers, Latinx workers were also dying, and the companies were not saying any of those workers' deaths. There was not a report of any of those workers dying." The devastation from COVID could be seen at Friendship Cemetery in Springdale, which was dotted by the freshly dug graves of Marshallese poultry processing workers.

Although Magaly had hoped Marshallese workers would join Venceremos, they did not: "The Marshallese lost so many workers. They were the most affected, but nobody really talked about it. It is hard for us to get into that community. Without Venceremos, it is pretty much everybody keeps gatekeeping the workers not to be exposed to journalists, reporters, lawyers—nobody." As of July 2020, COVID had killed sixty Arkansas residents, half of whom were Marshallese. To put that data in perspective, the Marshallese make up 2 percent of the population in Arkansas, but by July 2020 represented 19 percent of the COVID cases.

....

In the fall of 2020, Tyson gave all fifteen hundred workers at Víctor's plant on Berry Street a COVID test, and a nurse told him the result was negative. He asked for a copy of the results, but the nurse said, "You are fine. Why do you need it?" He replied, "It is my right to request it," but he never received a copy. "They didn't give copies of the results to anyone," Víctor said. Some Tyson workers heard the results from nurses two weeks after taking the test. Víctor asked, "Why call and tell someone you're positive if they were already two weeks infecting other people and some people died?"

"Most people are afraid of being fired," Víctor went on. Tyson employed various techniques for firing workers. Víctor said that if they fired someone for being a "bad worker," it was hard to get another job. He continued: "It will be difficult to get other companies to contact you. They will always ask you where you worked, and when you say Tyson, they will communicate with them and [Tyson will] say that person is bad. They try to make you look bad so nobody will hire you. That is what people are most afraid of."

If Víctor became infected with, or died, of COVID, he knew getting Tyson's workers' compensation to cover his medical expenses would be an ordeal. He said, "They will ask you millions of questions with the intention of not paying you. After all those questions, they send you a form with the same questions they asked on the phone.

"They are exploiting us in a manner that is unjust and inhumane. We are expendable. Others will arrive," said Víctor. He mentioned a program Tyson had recently launched called Helping Hands, which encouraged workers to donate part of their paycheck to help other Tyson workers affected by COVID. "Oh, God, why do they do that?" he asked. "It's as if they were making fun of us," he added, noting that a company that makes billions of dollars should not ask workers to contribute to covering the cost of COVID infections.

The families of those who died from COVID could apply for Helping Hands funds via a third-party emergency assistance foundation based in West Palm Beach, Florida. Veronica, who helped manage the fund at the foundation that was a Tyson contractor, explained, "Every grant payment at the end of the day had to go through me." Veronica asked that her real name not be used to protect her from retaliation. She helped manage over three hundred funds for different companies, during the years she worked at the company.

Tyson donated money to a 501(c)(3) foundation, and the foundation administered the funds to the workers. "The IRS allows these very profitable companies to throw money in a fund, and it is tax-free. Companies donate money to get the write-off, and it is an employee benefit," said Veronica. Companies decided what benefits they wanted their employees to have. Veronica felt that what companies elected was indicative of the company's culture. When texting, Veronica and her co-workers referred to the Helping Hands funds as "death checks."

Veronica said that, compared to Tyson, which offered $1,500, Target offered payments of up to $4,000 to cover the funeral expenses of employees who had died of COVID. She said, "I compare these wealthy companies and what they did for their employees as compared to Tyson. Most of these companies are making money hand over fist, and they are using this as a tax write-off."

At night, Veronica lay awake worrying about the families of Tyson workers who died of COVID. She said, "These kinds of expenses cripple people."

Tyson offered the online form to request the COVID death funds in English, even though workers spoke dozens of other languages. Tyson could have provided the form in more languages, but they would have had to pay more to do so.

Veronica spoke rapidly as if she were out of breath: "The fact that a Tyson worker dies and their family gets $1,500 [which] doesn't even cover cremation. I remember late at night,

I would think, 'Forty people died today!' People went through utter despair," she said.

Sighing, Veronica continued, "This is the most egregious thing I saw, and it kept me up at night."

....

In April of 2020, workers, coordinating with Venceremos, petitioned to request higher pay from Tyson due to the dangers of working through the pandemic. Workers passed around the petition at work and secretly signed it. But someone reported to a manager that Víctor had signed it, and he was called into the office. The manager said, "Someone said you were doing things inside that you shouldn't be doing. You were inside getting signatures on a petition, and you got colleagues to abandon their work to sign it."

Víctor responded, "Look, that petition—it's all true. Everything I read appeared true, and I signed it. When they gave it to me to sign, I gave it to another worker, and they gave it to another worker. I don't know where it came from or where it ended. It just arrived in my hands." Since they couldn't prove anything, Víctor wasn't punished. "They haven't even raised pay five cents," he said, sighing.

When Gloria and her co-workers approached their supervisor with worries about COVID, she said, "They say you got infected at fiestas. The managers [would say], 'I don't know where you got it, but it was from parties.' Every holiday they tell us not to have fiestas. Nobody is going to have parties in this situation." Gloria noted that supervisors at her plant consistently told workers that they were bringing COVID infections into the plant—that it was their irresponsible behavior in their few hours a week outside of work causing massive COVID outbreaks at Tyson plants. "We don't have support from anyone. They can do what they want," said Gloria of Tyson.

Despite the increased line speeds, the lack of workers due to COVID infections and deaths, and record-breaking profits, Tyson did not raise wages in 2020. "They didn't want to increase wages. We were earning the same," said Gloria. Venceremos, with Gloria, Víctor, and others, had worked so hard and risked so much to circulate the petition asking Tyson for COVID-related protections and pay. But Tyson didn't respond.

Like his co-workers Gloria and Víctor, Plácido was worried about COVID and money but glad to have the support of his youngest son, Darío, who was born in El Salvador and had migrated to the US in 2013. Darío, who was undocumented, worked construction and woke up at dawn each day to carpool an hour to work in Van Buren. He had pale green eyes and a soft voice and moved slowly and deliberately.

Born shortly after Plácido met Angelina, Darío said of his parents, "I didn't know them. They left me."

Angelina explained, "He was fifteen months old. We left him with his siblings."

Sitting at a small round table eating a pupusa, Darío said that his father was constantly sick.

Angelina added, "He is sick, and his feet are swollen. He has a fever and takes medicine to be able to work." Plácido was afraid Tyson would punish him with points and then fire him. "He went to work with a fever. Look how he suffers. My husband suffers too much."

Darío, pointing down the hall to the bathroom, said, "Sometimes he cries alone there."

"He cries," Angelina confirmed, putting a plate stacked with pupusas on the table.

"He thinks nobody is here before he goes to work, and he cries in the bathroom," said Darío.

Angelina put more hot pupusas on the plate on the table. His doctor had told him that he shouldn't drive alone. "That is why he cried because he knew he would die. And then the illness arrived," said Angelina. Predicting his death to one of his grandchildren, Plácido explained, "The ammonia put an end to my lungs." But he had to keep working during the pandemic, even though he knew the virus could kill him.

"Out of necessity. He had to work. He had to pay for many things, right? He had to work," said Darío softly, his eyes on his plate.

"He sends money to his brother," said Angelina.

Angelina mused: "He said next summer let's go to El Salvador if I'm not dead yet." Plácido wanted to visit his brother in El Salvador but said, "I don't think I will see him." The doctor had told him only a tiny piece of the lung was functional.

8

ABSENCE IS A SILENT PAIN

By March of 2020, Plácido was afraid to report to work because of the lack of COVID precautions and the high infection rates among his co-workers. The following month, unbeknownst to Plácido and other Tyson employees, the CEOs of the three largest meatpacking companies—Tyson, JBS, and Smithfield—had a meeting with Secretary of Agriculture Sonny Perdue. They requested that he "elevate the need for messaging about the importance of our workforce staying at work to the POTUS or VP level." A talking point that meatpacking representatives prepared was titled "Unemployment Benefits Should Not be Provided to People Who Quit Their Jobs." Meatpacking representatives argued that "being afraid of COVID-19 is not a reason to quit your job." They wanted to ensure workers like Plácido knew they were not eligible for unemployment compensation if they quit. As a result of the meeting, Vice President Mike Pence held a press conference in which he called on meatpacking workers: "We need you to continue ... to show up and do your job," noting that absenteeism was not acceptable.

That March, as the same meatpacking companies lobbied

USDA officials, they also pressured the U.S. Department of Labor to refuse to provide benefits to workers who chose to stay home or quit work due to fears of contracting COVID. In an email, a meatpacking lobbyist wrote to a USDA official, "so [USDA] can educate the Department of Labor on how to develop rules that apply to the Coronavirus Aid, Relief, and Economic Security Act [...] and the Families First Coronavirus Response Act [] in a way that does not incentivize our workers to stay home instead of coming to work."

Immigrants like Plácido make up roughly 40 percent of America's 470,000 meatpacking workers. According to a CDC report from July, 87 percent of the cases that occurred at meat and poultry processing facilities in April and May involved non-White workers. By June, Tyson reported that 13 percent of its workers in Northwest Arkansas had tested positive for the virus.

Although many immigrant workers at the Berry Street Plant had, like Plácido, existing health complications due to the chemical accident that would put them more at risk if they got COVID, Tyson executives decided to justify keeping plants open and pressuring employees to work. The company, its managers, and its public relations team claimed that a protein shortage would overtake the United States if Tyson didn't continue to operate. The top meatpacking companies often appeared to work together, coordinating messaging to keep plants running. Kenneth Sullivan, the CEO of Smithfield Foods, one of the top three meatpacking companies in the US, claimed that closing facilities would result in "pushing our country perilously close to the edge in terms of our nation's meat supply."

Plácido, who shared his health worries with his supervisor,

was told that he needed to continue to work to "feed the nation." As he continued to work, Tyson and other meatpacking companies spent the month of April lobbying the White House not to enforce any COVID safety rules that would impact the productivity of meatpacking plants. In an April 9, 2020, email to an aide to Vice President Pence, a meatpacking industry representative requested "intervention with governors, local officials and some indication the [White House] is saying that we need and expect plants to keep operating even with COVID-positive tests."

Víctor, listening to the radio, as he did every morning, had a strange experience. He heard an official from the Arkansas Department of Health announce that workers from any company could not be forced to work with COVID. The official asked listeners to call him and report such violations. Víctor wrote down the number and called. A woman answered the phone, and Víctor told her: "Where I work, there are many people infected, and the company is forcing them to work because they don't have symptoms. Could you help me with this?" In response, she asked him where he worked. When he replied, "Tyson," she said he needed to call a different number. "I didn't call it," said Víctor, worried that the health department might collude with Tyson to identify workers who were speaking out. Víctor had hoped to talk with the health department official about how Tyson was testing workers for COVID. He said, "If the CDC says that any person who takes a test has to wait at home until receiving the results in two to three days and can't work, why did these guys here give the test and tell us to go outside and take the test, and then we returned to work? It is a spectacle, nothing more."

. . . .

On April 13, public health officials ordered JBS to close a meat-packing facility in Greeley, Colorado, after a COVID outbreak. That same month, meatpacking company representatives met with the USDA and the White House. The companies were worried about more plants being forced to close because of state and local public health measures. An industry representative complained that "the media reporting is going to create more attention from health departments and governors in other communities IMO [in my opinion]. It seems to be cascading, and our friends at [the] USDA and the VP's office are not able to stop it."

In response to challenges from journalists and health departments, Tyson and Smithfield proposed an executive order to protect meatpacking companies from COVID-related lawsuits and exempt them from oversight by state and local health departments. A draft of the order was written by Tyson's legal department and shared with USDA officials. The Tyson draft of the order stated: "I also recognize that other industries play a crucial role in supporting the Nation throughout this emergency, including those critical infrastructure industries, as defined by the Department of Homeland Security, such as food production and supply. Businesses operating in the food supply and production industry have a special responsibility to maintain, to the fullest extent possible, their operations and normal work schedules."

Tyson and Smithfield representatives communicated constantly with Trump appointees at the USDA and the White House before President Trump signed the executive order. For example, Tyson CEO Noel White was on a call with Vice President Pence's Chief of Staff Marc Short, and he suggested that the order refer to the Defense Production Act of 1950 to ensure that meatpacking plants could continue to operate despite COVID outbreaks. During the first year of the pandemic, Tyson and Smithfield facilities were the site of thirty-nine thousand COVID infections among workers, resulting in the death of at least 176 workers.

Like other top meatpacking companies, Tyson lobbied for liability protection as meatpacking workers began to die of COVID. In April 2020, as reports of coronavirus outbreaks at meat processing plants piled up, President Trump spoke in favor of liability protections for meatpacking plants. This fulfilled a dream expressed by a Tyson government relations executive earlier that month that meatpacking companies would not have to face legal liability: "I realize this exe[cutive] order is a long shot, but my legal team really wants some type of protection from the plaintiffs' bar."

Such protections made it almost impossible for workers to sue meatpacking companies for being infected with, or dying of, COVID while on the job. The meat processing industry spent weeks lobbying and made critical donations to President Trump in the run-up. Later that month, the president classified plants as critical infrastructure.

Meatpacking workers have had little recourse to hold meat processing companies accountable for failing to institute adequate safety measures against COVID. In part, that's because Arkansas and more than a dozen states took steps to limit COVID-related civil liability for meatpacking plants and other businesses. Such shields make it difficult for the families of workers who die from the virus to sue the companies who operate the workplaces where they believe they contracted the virus.

Those who support limited liability argue that it encourages the reopening of the economy by protecting businesses from lawsuits. For meat processing plants, these liability shields have been used to guard against workers' compensation claims that could drive up the cost of insurance premiums and cut into profits.

....

One day in June of 2020, Plácido felt sick at work and was too weak to continue. He was sent home and spent a week in bed. Angelina said, "I fed him, but I didn't know that he had already become infected at Tyson." Plácido's body hurt, and he wondered if he had "that illness," but Angelina had already spent the whole week near him, as had other family members. Plácido was hospitalized in Fayetteville with COVID-19 on June 4. But the hospital sent him home for reasons Angelina didn't understand. "They didn't want to care for him," she said.

When he returned home from the hospital, he complained that his lungs were about to give out. He felt hot and took a freezing cold shower—something he never did, noted Angelina. He laid down and said, "I feel like I'm drowning." Angelina knew he was in agony and called her son to take him back to the hospital. Before her son arrived, an ambulance pulled up, and men came to the door to get Plácido. Angelina said that nobody in her family had called the ambulance, and she didn't know why it had arrived. "They took him in his boxer shorts. They didn't even let him put on clothes. But when they took him, he was already purple. Then he died in the ambulance, but they brought him back to life at the hospital," said Angelina. Upon his arrival at the hospital, Plácido was put on a ventilator.

"Everyone got it," said Angelina. Their oldest son, César, who is forty-four, spent three months intubated. By December of the same year, her son was out of the hospital, but Angelina said, "César is going to die because he is swollen, and his feet are swollen."

Ten of his family members, including Angelina, were infected with the virus while helping to care for him. They would recover—Plácido did not. After watching her unconscious husband suffer for two months, Angelina said goodbye to him over video chat. On the night of July 2, 2020, he died of COVID.

A few days after Plácido was first hospitalized, Angelina tested positive for COVID and was taken to a hospital in Rogers. Dario got COVID, too, but he was afraid to go to the hospital since he was undocumented.

Magaly, who supported Angelina in the aftermath of Plácido's death, said, "For the companies, it was, as Angelina says, 'I went to notify them that my husband died, and it was as if I had informed them that a dog had died.'"

. . . .

As soon as Angelina recovered from COVID that July, she gathered money for Plácido's funeral. First, she went to speak to someone at Tyson to see if they would help pay for the funeral. "They said they were sorry but didn't even give me a single dollar. They are insulting and have no compassion for the people who work there," said Angelina. She looked at the photo she had taken of Plácido's deathbed, remembering how she saw him on a screen. She said of the image, "I took it at midday, and he died about eleven p.m. It was very sad, but thank God, we could bury him. I got $3,000 together to cover it. Thank God, I covered it. My son helped me pay for it."

Walking around the house after his death, she pointed out

things he did and liked: "He bathed here. His favorite shampoo was that one. He slept there, and that was his favorite blanket. There is the talcum powder he put on his feet." Looking out the front window, she pointed to his green car with the metallic sheen of June bug wings.

Angelina talked about her brujo. In the first year of the pandemic, she paid him monthly, a total of $3,000. After Plácido's death that same year, she enlisted the brujo's help to make Tyson "vomit money." In Arkansas, she was unlikely to find a lawyer willing to take on Tyson for labor rights issues, so she and the brujo did what they could. Angelina believed in God's power, witches, and lawyers, but she had more access to some mechanisms for justice than others. She didn't know any lawyers, but she hoped to find one.

The brujo, who lived in Siloam Springs, raised goats, and some of his work involved sacrificing them. Beyond that, Angelina didn't want to reveal his methods. She usually went to the casino to gamble when she visited the brujo. She and Plácido had gone together, and it reminded her of him. She said, "What he loved was the casino." And then she laughed, adding, "He loved the casino. Man, he was fascinated with it. It was his fun, the casino."

Siloam Springs, a town of seventeen thousand, was a twenty-five-minute drive from Springdale and is the headquarters of Simmons Foods, the poultry processing company where Angelina got a job after she was fired from Tyson. She made $19/hour, more than Plácido made at Tyson, which pleased her. But the work was the same, the rhythm and the demands, the standing all day. Her feet and ankles were often swollen.

In addition to visiting the brujo and going to the casino (which she did infrequently after her husband's death since she didn't know how to drive), she was, with Magaly's help, looking for a lawyer. She wanted justice for her husband and would figure out how to get it from Tyson.

Angelina said that Tyson knew that her husband initially got sick at work—what she considered his first death, the loss of his life as he knew it. His second death was due to COVID, but chemicals caused his first, and she said of the company, "Tyson knows everything. It's there in the documents, the hospital documents. He suffered a lot."

In her kitchen, behind a collection of miscellany and remnants of her life with her husband—including a push lawnmower, fishing poles, and a 3D clock showing the Last Supper—Angelina left a cup covered in red hearts full of fresh coffee for Plácido. On a cluttered altar of sorts, she arranged a glass of water and a shot of tequila beside the coffee for her husband. "He arrives in the night to support me," she said of his ghost. "And I make coffee because that is what he said he wants." When he was alive, if Angelina made him ten cups of coffee, he would drink them all.

On any given day, Angelina might talk about cooking or her children, but she always circled back to Plácido's death, telling and retelling that story and adding details.

Standing near the stove in plastic sandals, Angelina said that on July 3, 2020, in the early morning hours, she got up to go to the bathroom, and Plácido shouted at her. Angelina said, "He began to shout, three yells. It was dawn, and I didn't open the door, but he shouted three times to say goodbye to me. It was very sad." On July 2, when the hospital pronounced him dead, he had been on a ventilator for weeks. Angelina had a recurring dream that he was alive, in her arms, and she was caressing his head. "I dream that he is alive, thank God, because being dead has to feel bad," Angelina said.

"He said because of his work he would die," said Angelina.

Darío sat at the kitchen table next to a box of mangoes and said of his father, "We planted the garden—tomatoes, corn, beans …

He said to my son, 'Let's plant tomatoes. I won't live to eat them, but you all will.'"

Darío said, "He told me to take a photo of him sitting near his garden."

One Sunday in July of 2021, Angelina went to Bluff Cemetery in Springdale to visit Plácido's grave. When she arrived, she kneeled and laid her cheek on his tombstone. It features three hearts, the central and largest one is yellow and includes an image of her husband wearing a shirt printed with playing cards and a gold watch. The two hearts surrounding his picture read: "A dear husband, father, and grandfather. His absence is a silent pain, his life a beautiful memory. He will live in our hearts." And "Your life was a blessing. Your memory is a treasure … you are loved beyond words and missed immeasurably." Nearby, Angelina spotted Martín Barroso's tombstone.

…………

A black velvet bow hangs on the door of a small house on a quiet street in Springdale where Gabriel Barroso lives with his wife and two young children. Gabriel is no longer at Tyson, but his mom and two sisters still work for the company. It was October

1, 2020, and he was supposed to be celebrating his thirtieth birthday, but he was still mourning his dad, Martín.

His shoulders stooped, his eyes down; Gabriel said of his father, "I've lived without him June, July, August, and September—almost four months since he went to the hospital and never returned. My oldest child understands, but the youngest doesn't. They ask for him. They want him to come home."

Martín and his wife worked at the same plant as Plácido, as did two of their daughters. Gabriel said his dad wasn't afraid of COVID, and that he took precautions. After work, he stripped off his clothes and washed them. He always wore a mask to go out. Martín told Gabriel, "We don't know where we will get it, and if God wants, God will choose."

Gabriel said, "He was positive that if it was his time, it was time, and only God knows. He had bad luck."

On May 31, 2020, his wife woke up feeling sick and thought it was the flu.

She went to her doctor, not Tyson's, and took a COVID test. Martín had a cough but thought it was normal. He worked Monday, Tuesday, and Wednesday as his wife waited for her test results. She worked because a Tyson supervisor asked her to do so until she received her test results. She tested positive. Martín took a test at the Tyson plant the day she received her results. Tyson wanted him to keep working while he waited for his results, but his family wanted him home. He and his wife quarantined for a week.

One morning, she couldn't breathe and called an ambulance. By the afternoon, Martín had done the same. They both had COVID. Gabriel said, "At first, I didn't think it was so serious, but when you live it in your flesh, you realize it is serious."

The day Martín's wife was discharged from the hospital, her

husband was intubated. For four weeks, he couldn't speak. Tyson wanted verbal authorization from Martín to approve his medical leave paycheck. Doctors performed a tracheostomy, and Martín recovered enough to go to therapy.

Once Martín was hospitalized with COVID, his family made video calls to him, but he couldn't talk because he was on a ventilator. Gabriel said his family talked, joked, and prayed. His sisters visited Martín two days before he died. He tried to speak, but "we never knew what he wanted to say," said Gabriel.

Martín was released from the hospital to undergo therapy, but the tracheostomy in his neck meant he couldn't respond to his family. He could only listen. When his condition suddenly worsened, he had to be intubated and died.

Before his father's hospitalization, Gabriel had imagined COVID as something people got and recovered from. Of his father, he said, "We thought after two weeks, things might improve, but on a Monday, they got worse, and he couldn't breathe." His mother, who had gotten COVID from her husband, was in the emergency room. She felt so bad she had decided to go to the hospital. Gabriel said, "They said her oxygen levels were low. We returned, and my dad did the same; he felt his chest [get] tight, and [he] couldn't breathe. His oxygen was low, and he didn't look good." Gabriel and his family couldn't visit his father except via video call. "It was the saddest part that we couldn't be with him," he said.

He sat silent for a long time and then said of his father, "He wasn't a bad person. He didn't mess with anyone. He was happy. He was happy and smiling; those moments can't be repeated. Nothing will be the same. Like now, on my birthday, I remember last year he was here, and we were celebrating, and now I don't even want to celebrate or go out. Now he's not here, and it hurts."

Gabriel hoped Tyson would do the right thing but admitted that COVID wasn't over and more people would suffer. He said, "The best thing would be to do the right thing and not have cases like this [of workers who tested positive for COVID being requested to work], but they don't want to decrease production. For them doing the right thing will be difficult because they want to increase profits."

"Even crying doesn't make things return," Gabriel said. "It doesn't heal the wound. Family in Mexico, my grandma, and some of my dad's siblings. She has a tourist visa but couldn't attend my father's funeral. She wanted to say goodbye but couldn't."

Then, the bills began to arrive. Martín's widow couldn't work because she was suffering from long-term COVID. For his children, the truth is that they couldn't look at the bills. Sometimes, they ripped them up, throwing the pieces into the air. Martín's family wondered if things were different if he would still be alive.

Martín's daughters are convinced they got COVID working at Tyson, and then his three youngest children got it. By the end of the month, the entire family had survived it. The family pooled money to pay for Martín's funeral. A check arrived—it was Martín's life insurance. But they didn't want the money— they wanted him alive. Martín's wife used the check to pay for expenses for her youngest children, fifteen and twelve. "They aren't babies, but they don't work," said Martín's son.

But the bills kept coming, and Gabriel's family couldn't pay them. His home, filled with family, became a space of loss.

Gabriel couldn't even look at the bills: "He was in the hospital for two months. Twenty-four hours a day for two months, imagine it. Now, with all this and the funeral and expenses with all that happened with him, I stopped working some days, and they don't pay us, and the rent doesn't wait. How will we pay those bills?" The hospital hadn't called the house, but letters from the hospital kept arriving.

Reflecting on who was responsible, Gabriel said, "I think that more than anything, the company Tyson is responsible; what they did badly was that they didn't want to decrease production. More families have lost loved ones, and it is their responsibility." Another man who worked in the same area as his dad had also died of COVID.

Gabriel buried his father at a cemetery ten minutes from his house.

"You could say that Tyson killed that guy little by little," said Víctor in November of 2020 of Martín. At Venceremos meetings, Víctor and other workers wondered how they could achieve some measure of justice for the dead and what that would look like. Víctor was from the same town in Mexico as Gabriel, and they had known each other since childhood. He said, "It made me very sad when I realized Gabriel's dad died. He was only fifty-five. Physically, he looked very strong. How is it possible that he died?"

....

In November 2020, Víctor, Gloria, and a dozen more workers participating in Venceremos formed an initial group committed to a class action lawsuit. Magaly began to help the workers look for a law firm that would take the case.

Although Magaly wasn't sure when the lawsuit would be filed and become public, she considered returning to Mexico for her safety. She said, "With this legal process, whenever that happens, I will leave for a certain period."

Explaining why he would use the little free time he had to work on a legal case, Víctor said, "I cried because Tyson didn't care enough to prevent this. If they had done things right, nobody would have died. Tyson has all the resources to have avoided this. They have all the money, but they don't care. They could have spent money to protect people because they have a lot of money. They care more about chicken than people. If you throw a chicken or kick it, they will fire you."

At a December 5, 2020, vigil in Springdale for meatpacking workers who had died of COVID, Angelina Pacheco stood alone, her head down, as workers lit candles in memory of colleagues: Plácido Arrue, Raúl Camacho, Salvador Zamorano, Khammy Nothongkham, Alonso Rosa, Manuel Mandujano, Jesús Lavato Molina, Martín Barroso, Martín Arenas, and Viensong Phanphengdee. She said of Plácido, "That day, my husband had been really sick for a week. But we didn't know what he had. I went to bed, lay beside him, and fed him while he was sick. But he already knew he would die because the doctor told him that the ammonia from work … "

" … had affected him," Gabriel finished for her. He stood by Angelina to remember the two men who had survived the chemical accident at the Berry Street Plant in Springdale in 2011, but who had not survived COVID.

Magaly, who organized the vigil, said, "Many workers have a million medical bills, and indebted families of those who've died of COVID have faced threats of eviction." Yet these jobs are precious in immigrant communities, and people fear losing them. "These companies have done a tremendous job making workers afraid of even speaking up."

Chaplains and community leaders in Arkansas questioned Magaly's behavior, saying, "If you keep fighting the way that you fight, you're going to harm the workers. Nobody is going to support you." She knew that Tyson wanted to isolate her, so she tried to empower workers directly by teaching them skills to fight for their rights.

In December of 2020, Gabriel drove to Bluff Cemetery in Springdale. Even at the cemetery, there was segregation, and all the Latinx people were buried in one section that was more brightly decorated than the rest of the place. Walking toward Martín's grave, a bare patch of freshly dug ground with a small plastic marker decorated with colorful helium balloons and Mexican candy, he said, "I'm sad because it hurts like it was the first day. As I said, these are dates when you feel the pain more; every time a month passes since his death, like Thanksgiving, Christmas, when the family is together, his presence is missed." He was still receiving hospital bills related to his dad's COVID but couldn't look at them. Gabriel said, "With everything that happened, how will we pay them? I need to see if they are there, but we ignore them. I remember that one for the therapies arrived at $650,000." His dad would have been fifty-six in November 2020, and the family gathered on his birthday, even though they had nobody to celebrate.

The families of workers who died of COVID faced hundreds of thousands of dollars in medical bills and threats of eviction.

Overwhelmed by her husband's funeral expenses, Angelina said, "It fell to me to find the money to pay for the funeral." She asked family in El Salvador for donations, adding, "It is very sad, but thank God we are moving forward. People helped us a lot with the burial, and I received some money, a thousand dollars."

Magaly, while supporting the families of disabled and dead workers, noted, "Trump, with the executive order to allow these companies to be open, killed workers. The company argued that there was a meat shortage—there was no meat shortage in April 2020. There was no such thing. They used that excuse to increase prices. They were also exporting meat to China." In the months leading up to the executive order, Tyson had spent money on advertising campaigns calling essential workers heroes, arguing that they were saving the nation. Magaly said, "That sounds good, romantic, but it was nothing like that. We realized we were alone. If we didn't do anything, workers would die, and nobody would have known the impact of the pandemic. Corporate America failed its own people. The pandemic has shown us how the system is not working for the people."

. . . .

In the fall of 2020, Quetzali was in mourning. She wanted to visit Bobby. Hopping in her car, she drove wildly, hugging the curves in the road like a race car driver. Arriving at the cemetery where he was buried, Quetzali exited the car, threw herself down, and kissed the ground beside a grave decorated with purple and lilac plastic flowers and a tiny gold angel. She said, "I married him for love, not money." There was no tombstone yet, only a metal stake with a photo of Bobby juxtaposed with one of a fish. Quetzali wanted to be buried beside him, patting the ground, noting that his ex-wife was on the other side. She put her face up to the photo, looking at her husband, reminiscing about how much he loved fishing.

In April 2020, Tyson's supervisors told workers at some plant that masks were optional, and they could make their own. By May 2020, rural counties with meatpacking facilities, like the one where Green Forest was located, had nearly five times the number of COVID cases as counties without meatpacking facilities. The conditions at meatpacking plants had far-reaching effects, as workers spread COVID among their families—families that lived together in multigenerational homes—causing disability and death.

Quetzali went to work on June 12, 2020, and began to feel her body ache. She went to the on-site clinic and said she needed to go home because she felt sick. The nurse did not offer her a COVID test, and her supervisor threatened to give her a point if she left. Quetzali said, "I left without caring about the point I would receive that Thursday. But Friday, I had to return to work because they would add two points."

She and Bobby both experienced body aches at home after work. After a few days, Bobby, who had been cleaning box lids at Tyson, was hospitalized. A few days later, he died. "He couldn't survive it," Quetzali said of COVID. "He had endured so much. He had an eye operation, a heart operation, and skin problems. I have a record of it all. I took care of him. He wanted to live." Bobby's body lay at the funeral home for two days, decomposing. Quetzali was in the throes of COVID and couldn't leave the house to sign the permission needed to bury him.

Bobby died of COVID on June 18, 2020. Before the ambulance came to pick him up, he told Quetzali, "Take care, and if I don't return, fight. And they should give you something because I worked there for twenty-five years."

Quetzali wore a gold ring with a fuchsia stone on her ring finger that read "TYSON" in bold lettering. Bobby had chosen the stone for the ring Tyson gave all its workers to mark a decade of service. Quetzali said of Bobby, "I always dream of him, that he is sitting on the sofa, just sitting and nothing more. He tells me to keep moving forward and not to be afraid. And to go to my country, shouting 'Your family is there. Go!'"

After Bobby died, Quetzali was lonely, and her niece from Guatemala came to live with her. Quetzali wanted justice for Bobby and herself; her hands were stiff and twisted like tree roots. She began to figure out what that would look like.

9

THE ARMADILLOS

n the fall of 2020, Quetzali's hands began to keep her up at night. She was worried about them, Bobby's medical bills, and the vaccine. As Quetzali and the families of dead meatpacking workers struggled to cover medical bills and funeral costs, they wanted compensation from Tyson, where their loved ones contracted the virus.

Workers talked nervously about a lawsuit, as what started with a dozen participants slowly grew. They worried about being surveilled, followed, found out, and fired. Their schedule at Tyson was intense, and many worked overtime, making it difficult to meet. Víctor, who thought Magaly had found a lawyer, said, "The lawyers aren't from here. I don't know where Magaly found them. They are from another state."

In December of that year, Víctor shared a photo with me that he had taken at work inside the Tyson Chick-N-Quick Plant in Rogers where he now worked. A bulletin board decorated with sparkly lettering read, "BABY, IT'S COVID OUTSIDE." Víctor said that managers constantly blamed workers for bringing COVID into the plant, and the messaging was consistent with that attempt to blame workers for the high rates of COVID infections. In an email,

Mickelson, the Senior Director of Public Relations at Tyson Foods, explained the bulletin board: "This signage was created by a health services staff member to promote coronavirus precautions. While this particular sign was taken down after management learned of it, we believe the healthcare workers involved were well-intentioned, trying to creatively encourage awareness of and engagement with public health recommendations."

Víctor had not yet been infected with COVID, but on February 9, 2021, a co-worker he had been in close contact with tested positive for the virus. Tyson didn't inform Víctor of the news; instead, he found out via text from his infected co-worker. Víctor went to his supervisor to tell him he had been in contact with the infected employee for at least an hour and a half. Once again, he recorded the conversation. His supervisor asked, "Do you have symptoms?"

Víctor responded, "No, only this morning I had a headache, which disappeared. Today, I realized he didn't come yesterday and was infected. I am worried." But his supervisor doubted that he had been in close contact with the infected employee, saying, "You weren't so close, farther than six feet."

Víctor responded, "No, he was beside me." His supervisor wondered if Víctor had been near the infected employee for over fifteen minutes. Víctor stated, again, that he had worked with the employee for over an hour.

His supervisor argued he would have to review camera footage to ensure Víctor was telling the truth and said that his plan was "I mean nothing for the time being. If you don't have any symptoms now, you can continue working."

Since his supervisor wouldn't take his worries seriously, Víctor went to a clinic after work to get tested for COVID. He stayed home for several days while waiting for the results—he tested negative—and Tyson penalized him for those absences.

On June 14, 2021, Víctor arrived for his shift to find that all workers were required to complete a survey. He recorded the interaction. A human resources employee told Víctor in Spanish: "This is a survey. Go from question to question, answering on a scale of one to five. Do you have any questions? You will pick from one to five. Four is good, and five is perfect."

Víctor asked, "What is this about?"

The man from human resources responded, "It is only a survey to see what you think of your colleagues."

Víctor, confused, asked, "What do you mean what do we think of our colleagues?"

"What do you think of the work of your colleagues? Do they need to improve their work? Do they need to fix things?" the HR man responded.

Víctor wondered, "So that people don't quit?"

The HR man explained, "To see what everyone sees, where everyone works, what things need the most attention so that we can look at it."

Víctor said, "Wages are very low, and the work is hard."

The HR man said, "You can write that there. Okay, and when you respond, put what you want. It doesn't serve us if you put down whatever and don't reflect your thoughts."

Reading the following survey question, Víctor asked, "And what does this question mean—do the people at Tyson embody the company's values?"

"It is asking what you think of the members of Tyson here,

if they respect people and things like that, if they care about people," said the HR man.

As he looked over the survey, Víctor, growing more upset, exclaimed, "Why do they ask these questions if they know they don't treat us well? Who thought of this?"

And then the recording ended.

....

That summer, Angelina was also feeling angry at Tyson. When the lawyer representing the class action lawsuit participants flew from Ohio to Arkansas to interview her, she told him, "Yes, I want to include my name." She said that Tyson "already sent me to hell, and that made me mad. They laughed at me." Angelina didn't remember the lawyer's name, but she clarified to him that she wanted her name on the lawsuit. She said, "I told him my husband died because he got that illness there, and his lungs were already destroyed. And they know it, I told him, that my husband died because of that. Perhaps they already revised all the paperwork because they came here for me to sign the lawsuit. That is why they came here for me to sign the lawsuit."

Angelina walked through the kitchen, out the back door, and into the June humidity, to stand among the corn Plácido had planted. It rose far above her head, and she walked barefoot among the stalks. Looking at the sky, she said, "I haven't killed anyone or anything. I haven't done anything wrong," as if to explain the difference between her and Tyson Foods.

Angelina's and Plácido's youngest son, Darío, walked out the kitchen door, his eyes green in the afternoon sunlight, his face a patchwork of shadows. He said of his father, "We didn't have the same belief in each other as we should have. I arrived when he was older, and we didn't have time together. Yes, he was sick frequently because of the ammonia, and I took him to the hospital. He was in his room, and I was in mine, but I was awake." Once Plácido got COVID, he got sick and couldn't walk even before he tested positive. Darío said, "He called me to take him to the clinic. We went, and, at about four p.m., my nephew told me he had COVID. Yes, he was sick. I wasn't afraid, but I was there and probably already had it. That same day, he called us all. He told me he was very sick and that he was going to die. He told me, take care of your mom because I won't return."

Darío reflected that he didn't think his father had attended school: "I don't think he studied." For Darío, school had been boring. He learned to read a bit, but when he tried to read, his head hurt. Once Angelina and Plácido arrived in the US, Darío said, "They were both supposed to be deported. They arrived here and requested permission, and then they were sent to be deported. They didn't leave. They didn't want to go. They endured it all."

When President Trump was elected, Darío said his father feared being deported. "When he wasn't well, he was worried about President Trump." But then, smiling at a memory, Darío said, "He [Plácido] was entertaining. He had many grandchildren."

With his father, Darío mostly talked about work. Plácido's only advice to him was to never work at Tyson. "Better not to," he said to his son. The golden afternoon light fading, Darío said of his father, "I miss him a lot. I just bought that green car for him. Two months before he died, I bought it." But neither

Darío nor Angelina knows how to drive, so the car sits in the driveway, a reminder of Plácido's absence.

. . . .

On July 20, 2022, the law firm representing the plaintiffs in the class action lawsuit, sent a letter to the workers involved stating that the lawsuit would likely be filed and become public by March 2021. That June, Magaly reflected on the number of refugees working at Tyson's. She said, "We saw this crisis in Syria. In Arkansas, progressives thought, 'We need to be a home for refugees.' It sounds great that we support these people because they are in need. The US created that need."

Reflecting on her own experience, Magaly said she had had few opportunities, even as an immigrant with an education. She said, "Arkansas is a hostile place for immigrants, Black people, and refugees. We have a responsibility to educate them about labor conditions and their rights." She imagined that refugee organizations would place any refugee without an education or language skills in a meatpacking plant. And she was right; Tyson Foods did create partnerships with NGOs that supported refugees.

Standing outside her apartment in Fayetteville with the late June heat melting her makeup, Magaly said, "Filing a worker case is a struggle." She had been following the wrongful death lawsuit against Tyson in Waterloo, Iowa, and was in conversations with organizers there. Magaly told me, "These organizations told us that lawyers gave flyers to workers to get them to join the lawsuit. You cannot be open like that here. I've never been to Waterloo, but it is not the home of Tyson. Even if they have a presence there, they don't have so much control as they do here in Arkansas." The workers couldn't do something as basic as finding a lawyer to file a case against the company was impossible. "It is difficult to find a lawyer to fight these companies in Arkansas. I have to search outside Arkansas," said Magaly. She found lawyers willing to take the case, and they came to Arkansas and interviewed workers. "They knew that there was a case," she said.

Magaly believes companies should not be able to do whatever they want with no accountability. The lawsuit alleges that workers suffered emotional distress from the work conditions during the pandemic. "This case is moving slowly because it involved interviewing workers from Springdale, Rogers, Van Buren, and Green Forest and hoping that other workers will join once it is public," explained Magaly. Unlike in Waterloo, she couldn't publicly look for workers to join the lawsuit because doing so would open them up to retaliation.

The general outlines of the lawsuit involved the COVID deaths of workers due to Tyson's negligence. Discussing the lawsuit, Magaly said, "I think they are trying to make the case that Tyson knew what they were doing and didn't stop. It is about negligence. They allowed this catastrophe to happen. And they had a responsibility to stop that, and they didn't do anything. They exposed workers to sickness and death." The lawyers needed time to gather information about working conditions, line speeds, the use of chemicals, and issues like the lack of bathroom breaks.

Magaly alerted the lawyers to investigate the on-site clinics at Tyson and the company's control over workers' health. She said, "I think that it's fraudulent that the last thing Tyson did was to expand on-site clinics and hire more nurses. Everybody was like, 'Oh, wow, Tyson is so good.' Because they don't know that the company uses this to control workers' health. Tyson or any other meat processing company should not hire nurses to take care of workers. That should be independent." Just as Tyson had vertically integrated every aspect of animal production, from feed to hatcheries to slaughter, the company wanted to control every part of workers' lives, especially their health. Wielding such control allowed the company to cut costs with little oversight of their treatment of workers or animals.

The week prior to our conversation, Magaly had met with a Tyson worker who had an accident at work and couldn't move her hands. Magaly said, "The doctor said that she is perfectly fine. She cannot see her own doctor outside of Tyson—because they are threatened with losing their job if they seek their own help. She could see the doctor of her choice if she paid the medical bills herself, which, for many workers, wasn't financially possible." Wondering what Tyson would do if a doctor said that many Tyson workers were sick and unable to work, she mused that doctor would lose their job. Nurses are placed in an uncomfortable position where they want to provide the best service possible but face conflicting pressures. Magaly said of a doctor who regularly treated Tyson workers: "He is loyal to the company. That is why the workers don't trust doctors. They often feel like anything that happens, they will only receive Tylenol or ibuprofen. Even if they feel like they cannot move their hands, it is the only thing."

The on-site nurses at Tyson witnessed Rosario's physical decline after the accident. Magaly said, "Rosario developed asthma and respiratory problems. You can hear her voice. She can't always stand by herself. The doctor saw the progression and how her health is worse every year. When the doctor had to provide results for the worker's comp benefit . . . he said she never got sick from the chemical accident—that she had asthma." Magaly was upset and called a lawyer to ask how Tyson could control a worker's health to such a degree, pronouncing individuals who had gotten sick at work to be healthy or sick due to a condition unrelated to work. Rosario changed doctors, but she felt paranoid and worried that no member of the medical profession would ever tell her the truth. Magaly said, "With Plácido they lied about his condition until he changed doctors. I speak with journalists about this issue because there is no investigation or related research. It's difficult to contact the nurses at those plants."

Even the lawyers had trouble finding Tyson on-site nurses to speak to them. With COVID, Tyson expanded on-site clinics, to which Magaly responded, "We don't need more! Where do they get these nurses from? Who would take that job?"

. . . .

On August 17, 2021, Magaly and I drove from Springdale to Rogers to visit Rosario at her house. We sat together in her sunlit kitchen, talking, and Magaly asked about her health. Rosario sat at the kitchen table, a row of small potted cacti behind her, and said, "Very bad, increasingly worse. I have chronic problems, like asthma. I am injured for life." Magaly wondered if, after the 2011 chemical accident, Tyson had paid Rosario's medical bills. Rosario told her, "Tyson is corrupt and paid for what was convenient and not what was inconvenient. They sent me to collections, but I don't know what happened to those bills. They didn't even pay for part of the bill." A decade later, Rosario still spent part of her salary on medications for issues related to the chemical accident. She was applying for government assistance to help cover medical expenses and continued hospital visits. Given her tight budget, her doctors gave her samples of medicines that they knew she couldn't afford. Rosario said of Tyson, "They aren't helping me. They injure you more each day. My medical bills grow, and it is their fault. I still receive many hospital bills. They don't care about workers. They want to get rid of anyone who doesn't serve them anymore."

On March 19, 2020, Rosario's doctor had advised her to request that the human resources department at Tyson's move her to an area of the plant where she wouldn't have to interact with chemicals. Rosario tried but said, "They said they couldn't accommodate me in any other area. The lady at human resources only laughed. And the nurse got annoyed. They said they couldn't give me work in an area without chemicals because the whole plant used chemicals."

Rosario said, "Chemical use is out of control. When we notify supervisors about it, they get annoyed."

Rosario had spent over a year at home, unable to work or breathe normally. She lamented to Magaly, "I can't do anything because I cough a lot, and it is hard to breathe. I try to walk for ten minutes, but I feel exhausted. Even talking is hard. Everything is tough. They injure you in every way. They don't care. All they want is to increase profits. They don't care. Tyson is ruthless. It happens to all workers; once they are injured, the company wants to find a way to get rid of them."

Magaly asked, "Do you think they wanted to get rid of you?"

Rosario said, "Of course. They want to get rid of anyone

who is injured and can't work for them. I'm sorry I'm crying but remembering everything I have survived has been hard."

For all those reasons, as well as her deep-rooted sense of justice, Rosario had joined Magaly in helping to create Venceremos. The two sat facing each other, their faces soft, round, and full of emotion.

....

On August 3, 2021, Tyson announced that it would require most US employees to be fully vaccinated by October 1 of that year, or they would lose their jobs. But Quetzali, like many workers, no longer trusted the company to tell the truth about anything.

Víctor, who had met Quetzali through Venceremos, was also worried. He said, "I haven't considered getting vaccinated because I don't trust them. I'm not confident in the company because Tyson didn't provide information about the vaccine or its symptoms. They didn't tell us the vaccine type or symptoms." Víctor so distrusted the company that he asked Magaly if Venceremos could protest Tyson's requirement that all employees get vaccinated. Quetzali and Víctor wanted to get vaccinated, but Tyson had abused their trust many times.

Magaly found news coverage of the vaccination program lacking, explaining, "The way Tyson handled it was a catastrophe. It discouraged workers from getting the vaccine." She noted that vaccinated workers were forced to return to work immediately, and many of them got faint, dizzy, or sick and weren't allowed to go home. Others, who had witnessed workers fainting on the lines, were concerned and didn't want to get vaccinated.

Magaly understood why many workers distrusted Tyson's vaccination program and worried because they had underlying medical conditions that put them more at risk. "It's hard. A lot of workers are not getting vaccinated. Many workers have symptoms from the vaccine, and they must go to work the next day. Because of the whole point system, they cannot miss work due to vaccine symptoms," she said.

Víctor noticed that after co-workers got vaccinated, they were often absent from work for several days. The vaccinated co-workers he talked to regularly complained of sore arms and body aches. Tyson allowed workers who got vaccinated to stay home for three days without pay, but on the fourth day, they had to return to work or face losing points. Too many points led to automatic termination. Víctor related a story to demonstrate how he believed Tyson used automatic termination to get rid of people who were old or injured.

"Yes, recently, they fired a colleague, a guy who was seventy-five, and he hurt his knee," said Víctor. His friend, Francisco, got hurt at the end of a shift around ten p.m. The on-site clinic was closed. He was still in significant pain the next day, and so he paid out of his pocket to visit a doctor not approved by Tyson. An x-ray showed that he had a torn ligament. Returning to work, Francisco went to human resources to explain his work injury. The human resources employee wanted to know why he had not visited the on-site clinic or notified his supervisor at the time of the injury. But he had been injured so late that his supervisor had left, and the on-site clinic was closed. Although he wanted to share his x-ray results, the human resources employee said he had to visit a doctor approved by Tyson: "Our doctor has to see you."

Francisco drove to Harrison, about an hour and twenty

minutes from Springdale, to visit the Tyson-approved doctor. Harrison is the national headquarters of the Ku Klux Klan, and many immigrant workers like Francisco were afraid to go there. The town has a billboard that advertises WhitePride Radio.com and reads, "It's not racist to love your people." Upon entering the consultation room, Francisco was surprised to see an on-site Tyson nurse from the Springdale plant. After a cursory examination, the doctor told Francisco, "You are fine. You don't have anything." When Francisco returned to work, a human resources employee was waiting for him and said, "The nurse reported that the doctor said you are fine." Upset, Francisco pulled out the x-ray his doctor had given him and said, "I can't work; it hurts a lot." Víctor said Francisco's supervisor eventually gave him a different job where he didn't have to walk. Francisco, worried about his knee, tried to return to his doctor. But when he arrived, the receptionist said the doctor couldn't see him and didn't have an appointment for months. Francisco was surprised and wondered if the human resources employee, who had seen his x-ray and knew his doctor's name, had exerted some influence to make his doctor turn him away.

When he returned to the plant, the human resources employee said, "Look, Francisco, you went to this clinic and that one."

Francisco asked, "How do you know I was in those clinics?"

"We know," said the human resources employee.

Francisco confided in Víctor that he felt like Tyson was surveilling him. On-site nurses at Tyson made several follow-up appointments for Francisco with their approved doctor. When he missed work to go, Tyson counted those days as an absence. The human resources employee told Francisco, "You know what, Francisco, you have lost a lot of points."

Francisco replied, "You shouldn't have taken away points."

The human resources employee said, "But you missed days for appointments."

On the verge of tears, Francisco pleaded, "But you sent me."

After he was fired, Francisco decided to return to his home country, Mexico. Víctor explained that Tyson used their control of on-site and off-site medical services to deny workers coverage and then fire them, thereby avoiding covering medical expenses. Víctor said, "They use that strategy with workers when they want to fire them. They want you to quit. That is what they do with people. They have strategies to make a worker leave."

....

In October 2021, still mourning Bobby's death, Quetzali told the nurses at Tyson that her hands weren't functioning anymore. "All they did was put bags of ice here and here," she said, pointing to her wrists. "That was all. And back to work." Ten days later, in pain, she returned to consult with a nurse, begging for approval to see a doctor. "No, the doctor, no, he is too busy," Quetzali was told.

Her fourteen-year-old niece was now in school in Green Forest: "I tell her to study because I don't want to see her at Tyson; that is not an option. She can study and be someone and earn money intelligently, because in no time you die. You don't only die of coronavirus. You can die of cancer or an accident that damages your lungs."

Quetzali sometimes visited Margarita, who lived nearby. The

two had become even closer friends as they got involved with Venceremos. "I don't want there to be continued injustices," Margarita explained about her decision to join Venceremos.

Standing before a portrait of the Virgin of Guadalupe decorated with blinking white lights, Margarita told me the pain began in 2017. Like Quetzali, she blamed it on her time working in debone, one of the most physically challenging jobs. Her body still, she moved her hands as if on a circuit that ended in a forceful downward jab, cutting the wing cleanly from the chicken. She cut twenty-four imaginary wings per minute, which on one shift would total around fifteen thousand wings. "That is what injured my hand," she said. Carpal tunnel syndrome is more common among meatpacking workers than in almost any other job due to the repetitive tasks of cutting, eviscerating, washing, trimming, and deboning. Margarita began visiting the nurse to complain about her hand in 2017 and, after months of complaints, received little more than ice and Tylenol.

Although OSHA encourages employers to provide early medical treatment to prevent permanent physical damage, the administration doesn't enforce such recommendations.

In Margarita's case, the doctor to whom she was referred told her she needed carpal tunnel surgery. However, he added that he couldn't perform it without Tyson's approval. More months passed, and Tyson's nurses sent Margarita to see two additional doctors, who both said she needed carpal tunnel surgery. Even then, the surgery wasn't approved. Margarita was advised, in her words, by one of the "Tyson doctors" to take steroids and get cortisone injections in her hand. She was scared because the doctor told her that while the stopgap measures could reduce her pain, they might also cause diabetes. She accepted this risk because the pain was too overwhelming to bear. The injection also allowed her to continue working—if she missed too many days, she would be fired.

Roughly eight months after she made the initial complaint, Tyson approved Margarita's surgery. "They operated on me on a Friday, and, by Monday, I was working again because if I didn't return, they were going to put me on unemployment and give me half of my check," she recalled.

Quetzali was happy for Margarita but frustrated when she was denied requests to see a doctor despite months of visits to the nurse at the plant in Green Forest. The company delayed her access to medical care, proper treatment, and time to heal. Other workers, a former nurse, and federal investigations into the industry reveal that her experience is typical.

OSHA investigations found that plants delayed medical care for injured workers, and OSHA issued a citation in one case and hazard alert letters in four others in 2015 and 2016. OSHA also found that a number of workers were fired after reporting musculoskeletal disorders at the former plant, some on the same day they reported injuries.

A subsequent investigation of meat and poultry plants by the GAO in 2017 noted that workers in five states similarly reported problems with on-site medical care, including the failure of nurses to make referrals to doctors and delaying medical care, once for a worker with a fractured wrist.

OSHA guidelines advise companies like Tyson to rotate employees through such jobs to avoid musculoskeletal disorders. They also urge employers to provide early medical treatment to prevent permanent physical damage. Those things didn't happen for Margarita.

Sometimes, the pain in both hands would overtake Quetzali, and she would drop her keys and groceries, proclaiming, "Oh, Lord, help me, help me pick it up."

"I am fighting for an operation they don't want to give me," she said, sighing. A nurse at the Tyson clinic told her, "We aren't going to pay for anything." Quetzali, fed up, said, "I choose my health and my work." That day, she left Tyson and decided to drive to the hospital. "They gave me medicine for the pain," she said. An MRI revealed that she had carpal tunnel in both hands. But Tyson would not approve the operation, which meant Quetzali would have to pay for it herself. The doctor recommended she take three months off work, which she did, but it was stressful without her paycheck to deal with "my part of the food, rent, car, and everything that I pay."

"They keep telling me to wait," she said of Tyson, "because they need workers. They say we don't have time right now because we have many problems with coronavirus."

"Dead, my hands," Quetzali said, describing how she felt when her hands wouldn't do what she wanted. "It remains in your body and nerves because you see how long I've been processing chicken," she said.

In May of 2022, almost a year after her first complaint to the nurses, Quetzali was still waiting for approval for her surgery when there was an accident at work. Water fell into one of the giant fryers full of hot oil, and the resulting explosion injured several workers. A co-worker, Rosa, a single mother of two boys, was five months pregnant and was injured. Hospitalized, she had second- and third-degree burns over 40 percent of her body. Her family launched a GoFundMe page to raise money to support her. The page included a description of Rosa's ordeal: "She was airlifted to a burn unit in Springfield, we ask of our community and friends to help us with expenses and bills as she will be hospitalized and cannot continue to work. Gloria is beautiful inside and out, loving, generous, and kind. She is the best of us, and we ask you all to help our family in this terrifying situation. We ask to keep her and her children in your prayers as she recovers from this tragic accident. Anything helps and is appreciated beyond measure. God bless you all." Rosa and her family, afraid of retribution from Tyson, did not want to be interviewed, so the only record of the accident is on the GoFundMe page. Quetzali commented on Tyson's ability to silence workers, "They have everyone under their control."

Shortly after that, Quetzali received a job survey asking her to define her level of happiness. "How happy are you?" was the question. Quetzali wrote, "I want medical attention, not humiliation." She received no response.

And then she had to deal with a co-worker who touched her butt. She told him, "Don't do that, or I will file a complaint." In response, she said he tried to "stick two fingers inside," as if he could penetrate her clothes with the force of his fingers. When she complained to her supervisor, he refused to fire the man for harassment. "Now I know not to complain," she said, noting, "He's done it with others."

"I'm not afraid of them sending me back to Guatemala—I'm afraid of them killing me."

Quetzali, whispering, asked, "Can I tell you something?" Looking out the window, her eyes to the sky, she explained that, two months prior, piles of dead animals started appearing under her house. "One time, it was armadillos and, another time, raccoons. We got sick from the smell." Quetzali thought it was Tyson's way of warning her to stop what she was doing—to not participate in Venceremos and not be vocal about needing carpal tunnel surgery. After that, worried about safety, she sent her niece away. "I don't have anything, but one day God will deliver justice," Quetzali said.

10

THE LAWSUIT

"That lawyer, nothing," Angelina said as she pulled up her skirt to show a swollen leg. It was June 2021, and she needed a ride to the clinic to get an MRI. Exiting the house, she passed a pile of kittens nestled in her rose bushes, their eyes still closed. "Magaly came to me, and she said, 'I know good lawyers who are very far away if you want.'" The lawsuit began taking shape, but Angelina couldn't remember the lawyer's name. He was in Texas or maybe Alabama.

A few months after Plácido's death in July 2020, Magaly talked to Angelina about what she could do to try to get justice from Tyson. Angelina said, "She showed me what I could do. I said, 'I don't know anything about lawyers.'" As I drove her to the clinic for her appointment, she discussed the lawsuit.

When she met with the lawyer for the first time, he asked her to gather all documents, like medical records, related to Plácido's case. "I am suing them," she said, her feet wide, her stance firm. "He doesn't speak Spanish," she added. While she hoped to win, she said she would wait to see what God said. The case was possible because the lawyers were working on contingency, she said, adding, "How would I pay if I don't even have enough money for myself?"

Angelina didn't know how long the case would take. She guessed, "One year, two years." And then, looking out the car window into the distance, she said Plácido had visited her. "I got up at midnight to go to the bathroom. I wasn't afraid. I saw him standing there," she said.

Before entering the clinic, Angelina said, "I don't feel good after COVID. I feel tired, and my body aches." None of the employees spoke Spanish at the clinic, which was a few minutes from her house. She motioned to one of the women at the front desk that she needed help filling out paperwork. She spent long days on her feet processing chicken. Her legs, she thought, could be swollen for many reasons, most of them related to work. Exiting the MRI, Angelina wanted to go to the casino in Siloam Springs because it had the best buffet. She said that while she would never make a living wage processing chicken, at least at the casino she sometimes won money.

Angelina worried about Tyson and how they might retaliate against her but said, "If they send someone to kill me, I tell myself I've already lived long enough."

She went to her room and dug in a box until she found a large Ziploc bag full of papers. She pulled a letter out and asked me to read it to her: the document's first paragraph explained that the law firm would represent a class action lawsuit against Tyson Foods "based on Tyson poorly managing the response to the COVID-19 pandemic."

Angelina placed a manila envelope containing 385 pages of Plácido's medical records on her kitchen table among several bags of limes. A document dated June 4, 2020, written by one outside doctor, noted that Plácido had arrived complaining of shortness of breath: "He has multiple sick contacts at work with COVID-19. He has general malaise. No nausea, vomiting, diarrhea. He works at Tyson Berry Street Plant." On June 6, 2020, Plácido returned to Mercy Hospital. Another doctor who Plácido visited noted a "history of exposure to ammonia fumes" and wrote, "He notably works at Tyson Berry Street Plant. He separates pieces of chicken at work notes around six people have been sick has had possible COVID exposure."

Angelina felt at once alone and accompanied as she sought justice for Plácido. He visited her as a spirit, as a ghost. Together, from the world of the living and the world of the dead, they moved forward on the strength of the truth.

Like Angelina, other families of workers who had died or who became disabled due to COVID looked to Magaly for advice. By late 2020, a dozen family members of victims had discussed the idea of a class action lawsuit, although they doubted any lawyer in Arkansas would help them. While they knew a class action lawsuit could take several years to put together, the families were committed to the process. Angelina and the families of other workers who had died of COVID had suffered through the aftermath of Trump's executive order. The results of the order, which Tyson and other meatpacking companies had devoted time and money lobbying for, led to at least 269 worker deaths in the first year of the pandemic.

It had been tiring work coordinating the lawsuit, and Magaly feared that Tyson was having her followed. She said, "They probably hired someone to investigate me." Paranoid, she became more careful about what she shared in the media. "I don't share my personal life. My life has changed a lot." She had

172 LIFE AND DEATH OF THE AMERICAN WORKER

trouble sleeping at night and, afraid of being followed, bought a camera to install on the back of her car.

But she paid attention when a class action lawsuit was filed in U.S. District Court, Eastern District of New York in February of 2021 that alleged that twice as many Tyson employees died after contracting COVID than at any other meatpacking company. More suits would follow, those of the Arkansas workers among them.

....

When the Ohio law firm agreed to take the case, they sent a team to Arkansas to interview Tyson workers and their families. In September of 2021, Magaly said, "They are reviewing the workers' medical records." She worried about protecting workers during the legal process and wondered if Tyson would retaliate against her.

In October, the House Select Subcommittee on the Coronavirus Crisis released a report stating that during the first year of the pandemic, nearly sixty thousand workers were infected, and 269 died. Magaly said, "Tyson is in a tough position." She feared the company would retaliate against workers. At that point, Magaly and a dozen workers had been quietly collaborating with the law firm for almost a year—a time of fear and worry but one of hope, too.

"Angelina supports me. She told me el brujo is going to help us. I hope so because the workers deserve some *alivio*," said Magaly, referring to the witch who had cast a spell on the company. But Magaly trusted the law firm, which had significant experience winning class action lawsuits. She said, "The firm is powerful.

They have the money to fight Tyson." Regarding legal issues, Magaly believed that Tyson was intentionally drawing things out. Her eyes dark and shining, Magaly said, "I am excited about this. It's going to be big."

After witnessing the dismissal of wrongful death lawsuits against meatpacking companies, the lawyers approached the issue from a different legal perspective. They made it about the affliction of emotional distress, based on the theory that a company should be liable for making people sick and purposely avoiding safety precautions. A company could cause an unbearable level of distress for its workers. It would be challenging to win. Magaly said, "This is a different type of lawsuit than the ones that have failed in Iowa. This isn't about wrongful death. It's a lawsuit about moral injury."

In July, Angelina received a letter and put it in the Ziploc bag where she stored other important documents. "Oh, it is hard to be alone," she said, looking at a calendar on the kitchen wall. July 2 fell on a Friday, but instead of visiting her husband's gravesite or holding a mass in his honor at church, she would be at work processing chicken. She walked to her bedroom and came back with the letter. The first paragraph explained that the law firm would represent a class action lawsuit against Tyson Foods "based on Tyson poorly managing the response to the COVID-19 pandemic."

The lawyer, who came to Arkansas during the summer of 2021 to meet with Angelina and other workers, told her that Plácido's case was the strongest given that doctors not affiliated with Tyson had documented his condition for years and had mentioned Tyson and the company's role in Plácido's health issues in their medical notes. According to a letter the lawyer sent Angelina, the class action lawsuit would be filed by March 2022.

One of Angelina's daughters worked at the same plant as Plácido; her job involved driving a small machine to pick up sacks of salt that would be mixed into specific recipes for chicken products. "She says it is good that I am doing this because my old man would be alive if his lungs hadn't been damaged," recounted Angelina.

As the last days of March neared, Angelina was sad for two reasons: she had received no news about the lawsuit being filed, and she couldn't get time off work to take a trip with Venceremos to learn about labor organizing.

Before the Venceremos trip, Magaly visited Rosario at her home in Rogers, and they talked about the 2018 trip to meet the Coalition of Immokalee Workers.

Rosario talked about the CIW model: "They adopted a good plan of conduct; for example, the consumer listens to the worker. The consumer doesn't know the difficulties that the worker lives." Rosario thought most people couldn't imagine how agricultural and meatpacking workers suffered. From the CIW, she learned that if workers educated consumers, everyone would benefit.

Sitting in Rosario's kitchen, Magaly asked what she wanted consumers to know about labor conditions at Tyson. Rosario wished consumers knew about the number of injuries at plants and would buy food from companies that showed respect for safety. Rosario wanted consumers to choose their food based on how companies treated their workers.

Magaly asked, "In Arkansas, do you think there is a lot of support for workers? Do many people worry about workers?

Does Tyson have an outsized influence?" Rosario noted that Arkansas was a problematic state for workers to organize around labor rights because Tyson contributed money to schools, universities, NGOs, and artists—the company "has bought everything." Rosario explained, "We don't want to damage the plant; we just want them to be on the path to justice, for them to profit but also to be just."

....

Darkness gathered on the morning of March 30, 2022, sucked into a funnel from the sky to the earth. The tornado ripped through Springdale, injuring seven people and several homes. But it didn't stop Víctor, Gloria, their kids, Mateo, his wife, and their two kids, Quetzali, Margarita, and Magaly from boarding a plane to Florida. The kids whispered about the ocean, which they had never seen. Magaly organized the trip so poultry processing workers could witness what they had yet to see in Arkansas—the collective power of a worker-led movement. I joined Magaly and the workers on the trip.

Stepping off the plane in Fort Myers, the workers and I were engulfed by swampy, humid air. After picking up rental cars, we drove to Fort Myers beach to see the ocean. The children ran in fully dressed, splashing and whooping as the adults watched from the shore.

Magaly and the poultry workers drove to Immokalee, forty miles northwest of the Everglades. Most tomatoes Americans consume every winter are grown in the surrounding farmland. Immokalee is home to some twenty-four thousand people, mostly agricultural workers. The Venceremos group arrived at the CIW community center, a sky blue building that houses a Spanish-language radio station and sits across from a parking lot filled with school buses that transport agricultural workers to and from the tomato fields.

Chickens ran across the front yard as Víctor and Gloria surveyed the area as their kids pleaded for snacks. Clouds of dust billowed around as buses entered and exited the dirt parking lot across the way, and agricultural workers, drenched in sweat, stood in groups waiting for their day to begin.

Marielena Hincapié, the Distinguished Immigration Scholar at Cornell Law School and the former executive director of the Los Angeles-based National Immigration Law Center (NILC) and the NILC Immigrant Justice Fund (IJF), said of the trip the poultry workers took to visit the CIW, "Part of the beauty of bringing them to Florida is that there's nothing more powerful and more transformative than workers meeting with other workers and seeing what's possible. Organizing is hard, slow work . . . it doesn't happen overnight, you know. It's about relationship building, trust building, and most importantly, helping workers see and imagine a different reality."

During the three days of the 2022 trip, the workers gathered for breakfast, eating tamales and drinking coffee while introducing themselves.

The CIW began organizing in 1993, and, like Venceremos, it started with a few workers. Over the years, the CIW developed a worker-led model using protests and media campaigns to pressure retailers to source food ethically and encourage consumers to support just labor conditions. Sameer Ashar is a Clinical Professor of Law at the University of California, Irvine, where he directs the Workers, Law, and Organizing Clinic, explained the power of the CIW, "Coalition for Immokalee Workers is one of the few immigrant worker-centered workers and immigrant worker center organizations that has accomplished a great deal through creative organizing campaigns."

During a break between CIW workshops, I sat with Quetzali and asked her about her dreams. I liked to talk about dreams with them because poultry workers often dreamed of their loved ones who had died of COVID. I wanted to hear the messages their dead husbands, wives, or children sent to them in their dreams.

She joined the class action lawsuit: "They shout at us at work. Many died. I'm doing it for my husband." The lawsuit was not yet public when we traveled to Florida. Given the power of Tyson, workers wondered if the lawsuit would survive to become public. For many workers, the trip was their first time on a plane, their first time meeting immigrants, documented and undocumented, who had organized their way into a position of power, their first time seeing the ocean.

And so, I talked to workers about their dreams and their visits with brujos because in Arkansas, the only place they could find justice was in other worlds. Angelina asked her brujo to put a spell on Tyson and make them pay for the harm they had caused by killing workers.

. . . .

On the second day of the trip, Mateo stood near his wife, looking out to the horizon. He explained why he had joined Venceremos,

"My whole life, since I was a child, I have been bullied. It makes me upset to see people take advantage of other people."

A young woman with a shock of fire engine red hair walked up with twin girls holding her hands. She introduced herself as Thelma and offered to walk the kids to get popsicles at the corner store. La Michoacana, a well-known Mexican ice cream shop, had mango, lime, and mamey popsicles, and colorful ice cream in hot pink and blue colors. Her daughters were eight years old and just tall enough to peer through the glass of the ice cream display. They left the store with bright blue ice cream running down their hands. The Venceremos kids faced a similar challenge, their popsicles immediately melting in the hundred-degree weather.

Thelma Gómez, a community organizer with Migrant Justice, had traveled from Vermont with a group of dairy workers to learn from the CIW. As a teen, she began working at small dairy farms, in what she described as inhumane conditions: fourteen-hour days that started at four a.m. She was underpaid and subjected to sexual harassment. Gómez, who was initially undocumented, said that "nobody wanted to complain to the boss ... because sometimes the bosses would turn workers in" to be deported. She got involved in organizing after she became a mother: "I want my daughters to be strong, and I want them to see us march together."

Entering the CIW headquarters, Venceremos workers met Gerardo Reyes Chávez. He had worked at the CIW for twenty-three years and helped launch the Fair Food Program. He was born in Zacatecas, Mexico, and began working in the fields at age eleven. Under public pressure orchestrated by the CIW, McDonald's,

Burger King, Subway, and other large brands joined the Fair Food Program. It has since been expanded to Georgia, South Carolina, Virginia, Maryland, North Carolina, and New Jersey. The program has not only resulted in higher wages for tomato workers but also put in place a system for reporting abuse and sexual harassment on the job, measures to prevent wage theft, and education classes for workers to inform them of their rights. Of the five largest fast-food corporations in the US, Wendy's is the only one that has refused to join the program, claiming that all its tomatoes are sourced from greenhouses. Although Wendy's has argued that greenhouse work conditions are safe and fair to workers, investigations have revealed that greenhouse workers often have few protections. In 2016, the CIW launched a national boycott of the chain. Now, the group was organizing a march in Palm Beach, home to the chair of Wendy's board, billionaire and Trump supporter Nelson Peltz.

Reyes Chávez said Arkansas workers had been contributing their energy to the CIW since 2018, although they had been organizing for years before that: "Not under Venceremos, but in this process of looking for a systemic solution to their problems. They wanted to learn because they heard about the Coalition's Fair Food Program, and they wanted to see how we had achieved changes where the workers have the right to work free from abuse, violence, sexual harassment, and assault."

Behind the headquarters, the CIW set up a demonstration area. Víctor, Gloria, Mateo, Margarita, and Quetzali watched as agricultural workers used life-sized illustrated posters to teach those in attendance about labor rights in the fields. Because many workers were illiterate, the illustrations were important.

Roosters crowed as agricultural workers interacted with the crowd in a call-and-response form. He shouted, "What do we need?" Someone in the group responded, "Commitment!" And the presenter confirmed, "Yes, we can do so much together. Our colleagues have traveled so far to be with us. We aren't alone." And then he asked everyone to get up and follow him. He walked to the parking lot, pointed to a truck, and said, "Let's see the power of what we can do together." Agricultural, poultry processing, dairy, and construction workers gathered around the truck. "Can you move it?" someone shouted. The workers gripped the vehicle from below, lifted it, and moved it several feet from its original position.

Reconvening in the area of the presentation, an agricultural worker stood up and said, "We are not asking for a favor. We are asking for something that . . . each of us on this earth deserves—justice." As the presentation ended, a spiritual from the Civil Rights Movement, "I Ain't Gonna Let Nobody Turn Me Around," played over the speakers. Tamales were served, and a worker grabbed the microphone and shouted, "Remember, we, the people, are more powerful than any amount of money."

Ashar said of Magaly's work to get poultry workers to Florida to visit the CIW, "This organizer is saying that what we're trying to do, is, like, give them a sense of solidarity with each other and to grow their sense of accountability to each other and then their support for each other when they decide to speak out to the employers. And that's been the strategy of a lot of immigrant worker centers and contexts in which there is no unionization, and there's no prospects. I think part of it is like a pilgrimage, you know, and then trying to get inspiration and maybe some strategy and bringing it back."

"I thought what she was doing was interesting," Mateo said of why he had joined Venceremos.

Tall with broad shoulders, he was often silent but had a wry sense of humor and a booming laugh. Plants were divided into two areas, which he described as raw chicken and cooked chicken. "The raw chicken area is where people are most abused," he said. He described men in the raw chicken areas drinking and doing drugs while on the job.

Mateo sat under an outdoor tent at the CIW, drinking coffee with agricultural workers, saying, "This is a new experience for me. I haven't been able to sleep because I have been thinking of things I can do when I return." He told Magaly, who sat across the table from him, that he had already learned more than he had hoped. "My kids wouldn't leave me alone the first day because they learned what this was all about," he said of the workshops on labor rights. His wife didn't work at Tyson, but he said, "She supports me, and I'm thankful to her for that."

Mateo was upset about how workers were treated but felt he had to remain silent to keep his job. He told a story about Janet, a fellow supervisor. Workers had to request permission to go to the bathroom, and by the time they arrived at the door, Janet was leaning against it. "Be quick," she whispered. He described working at Tyson as "like a theater production."

Mateo recalled working at Tyson alongside prisoners employed by Tyson. "They don't discriminate," he said of company's hiring practices, laughing. He believed that Tyson sent "the worst chicken to the prisons."

....

To understand the relationship between prisons and Tyson, I contacted Zachary Crow, the executive director of DecARcerate, a nongovernmental organization that works to end mass incarceration in Arkansas. The NGO recommended I meet with Willis Johnson, who has a meditative presence and looks younger than his forty-one years. Johnson, a Black man incarcerated at age fourteen on a murder conviction in Arkansas, labored at the 16,500-acre farm at Cummins Unit, a prison in southeastern Arkansas that holds 1,725 prisoners. Because he was convicted of murder, he wasn't allowed to get a work release for Tyson. Only prisoners who haven't been convicted of a violent crime or tried to escape prison could get a work release. Johnson said many prisoners were eager to leave the grounds at Cummins and accept the risks of work at Tyson.

Johnson worked in the fields planting soybeans, corn, wheat, cucumbers, watermelons, and cotton. If he didn't work quickly enough, he would be ordered to wade into a ditch, where he sometimes fended off water moccasins. The venomous snakes, their bodies dark and thick, gathered in the brackish waters surrounding the fields. But the field riders—uniformed correctional officers in crisp blue shirts on horseback—wouldn't allow prisoners to kill Arkansas wildlife. Johnson said, "You have this officer sitting up on a horse with a gun. The point is you're always under the threat of the gun. At Tyson, you aren't under that type of threat, but there are other dangers. People lose fingers. I know it happens there. You're always aware of the danger, but there are different dangers."

Soft-spoken, Johnson discussed how slavery ended in Arkansas in 1865. In 1902, Cummins, designed as a prison for Black men, was founded at the site of two cotton plantations—the prison continued to plant and harvest cotton with prison labor. As Johnson described, "Arkansas—it's one of the last plantation states." The prison, also a working farm, was set up to fund itself so that the state didn't have to pay for it. Prisoners call the fields at Cummings "The Farm." The facility is in Grady, Arkansas, a town with a population of 317.

When Johnson was released in 2022, he began volunteering at DecARcerate. Johnson, who resides in Marion, Arkansas, said, "Black and brown people make up the majority of those workforces." Black people comprise 15 percent of the state's population but 42 percent of the incarcerated population. On any given day, driving by "The Farm," you can see men, mostly Black, in white prison uniforms and matching hats, toiling under the Arkansas sun and the watchful eye of guards.

Prisoners at Cummings Unit care for ten thousand chickens and two thousand cattle and plant and pick cotton, just as enslaved people did. The cotton plant flowers in a burst of white petals that turn yellow, pink, and blood red. When the petals drop to the ground, green pods and, later, white puffs of cotton emerge. But the plant's life cycle can't be separated from its historical significance. According to Crow, some Black prisoners at Cummins spend every summer in solitary confinement because they refuse to pick cotton for White men. Prisoners who refuse to work or don't work fast enough are sent to solitary confinement, known as the "hole."

Johnson said of his time laboring in the fields, "Twenty-six years incarcerated, and I never had a job that paid me anything." Johnson, who worked on the "hoe squad," noted that many Tyson chickens eat corn planted and harvested by prisoners.

Tyson's treatment of vulnerable workers became more evident during the pandemic, as workers died of COVID. During the pandemic, Arkansas prisons and Tyson facilities shared a unique distinction—they were the sites with the most significant coronavirus outbreaks in the country, and those who were infected and died were predominantly from Black and immigrant communities. Despite the rapid spread of the virus and CDC recommendations, prisons and Tyson facilities lobbied to keep workers in the fields and in the factories.

Tyson operates in four states that allow prisoners to be forced to labor without compensation: Arkansas, Georgia, Alabama, and Texas. Tyson employs prisoners via work release programs that place prisoners at various companies. According to Dina Tyler, the communications director for the Arkansas Department of Corrections, the first work release program opened in Arkansas in 1974. The imprisoned men who participated in the program made at least minimum wage, and they reimbursed the state and paid court fees from their earnings. "They typically fill jobs that are hard to fill," said Tyler of the imprisoned men who worked at Tyson. "They work a regular work week, but sometimes they work overtime. The only difference is they spend the night at correctional facilities," Tyler added.

Zachary Crow, executive director at DecARcerate, reviews agricultural purchases at the Arkansas Department of Correction each year. Crow said, "Arkansas is like a handful, one of a couple of states that pay $0.00. And they say work is optional. But if you don't work, you get sent to solitary confinement." Crow noted of Tyson, "They're buying a ton of corn from the prison." Tyler, the communications director for the Arkansas Department of Corrections, confirmed that

Tyson Foods purchased $109,807.23 of corn in 2020 from correctional facilities and $921,300.24 in 2021.

Arkansas and Florida were the first states to pass "right to work" legislation that obscures its implicit goal of preventing unions and weakening labor rights. In 1944, when most meatpacking workers were Black, Arkansas legislators proposed the right-to-work amendment to ensure White workers would not organize with Black workers. Groups lobbying on behalf of the legislation, like the Arkansas Farm Bureau Federation and the Christian American Association, said that if the bill didn't pass, "White women and White men will be forced into organizations with Black African apes ... whom they will have to call 'brother' or lose their jobs."

In the 1960s, as the Civil Rights Movement gained force and focused on labor rights, Black workers began to organize and gain power. In response, meatpacking companies started looking for vulnerable workers to replace them, thus ushering in the era of hiring immigrants, refugees, the undocumented, participants in rehab programs, former cult members, and children. At the same time, meatpacking companies began to move factories from big cities like Chicago to small, rural towns. Companies realized they could influence local and state politics, creating an anti-union environment where they could pay workers less. They could also isolate workers, many of whom were undocumented and didn't speak English, from support networks. What were once stable, high-wage union jobs became positions where a meatpacking plant could experience over 90 percent turnover in any given year.

Distances between rural plants made labor organizing more difficult. I sometimes drove three or more hours to remote towns like Green Forest to interview plant workers across

Arkansas. In cities like Clarksville, where hundreds of workers were Myanmar refugees of the Karen ethnic minority, few people in town spoke Karen.

Zachary Crow said of the Arkansas Department of Corrections: "They were insistent on getting people into the field because they have a financial interest to make people work. While correctional officers who tested positive were sent home, prisoners who tested positive were required to continue their unpaid labor." The Cummins Unit was the site of the tenth largest COVID outbreak in the country. Data shows that imprisoned people and meatpacking workers suffered some of the highest rates of COVID infection during the pandemic. As of June 2020, of the two thousand imprisoned people at Cummins, primarily Black men, 956 had tested positive for COVID. Cummins sends imprisoned men to work at Tyson via a work release program.

A strange detail, said Crow, and one that he couldn't forget, was that prisoners—even those who tested positive for COVID—were asked to sew eighty thousand masks for prisoners and officers at facilities across the state. Similarly, Tyson workers at several Arkansas facilities reported being asked to sew their masks during the first months of the pandemic.

Reflecting on why imprisoned people continued to work at Tyson, Johnson said, "It is being able to get paid vs. not getting anything. Tyson looks like a savior."

Johnson was released from Cummins Unit in 2022, having been imprisoned for over half his life. Sitting in a Little Rock, Arkansas, coffee shop in April 2023, his face soft in the late afternoon light, he said to me, "The one thing that kept me going—and inspired my writing—is linking, you know, whatever struggles I may have been going through were the struggles that my ancestors were going through." He wanted to write a book about his experience tracing Cummins from the land where enslaved people picked cotton to The Farm where he and others labored, unpaid, to cultivate crops for Tyson and other companies.

....

Sitting near Mateo at the CIW gathering in Florida, Víctor said that he knew the fight to change labor conditions at Tyson would be challenging. He said, "If Magaly wants to continue, it won't be easy. We are in their territory." Like the CIW, Víctor proposed that Venceremos needed to pressure the consumers who bought Tyson products. But he also wanted Venceremos to educate the state government and public schools about labor conditions at the company because Tyson sold and donated chicken to both institutions. Víctor added, "We make roasted chicken for the prisoners. It is all bad quality," noting that prisons should be included in any campaign to bring awareness about Tyson's labor practices.

Víctor complained about the quality of nuggets and breaded chicken sent to schools. He said, "The nuggets and the breaded chicken are for schools. They don't care if the product is contaminated. Recently, it has been full of weevils. The school districts in this country should investigate this issue. The chicken is horrible."

Mateo, joking, announced in a booming voice, "Today is Friday! Today, we will make chicken for the prison!"

Víctor, pensive, changed topics, bringing up how Tyson blamed workers for accidents. "If something happens, they quickly create a legal document and make you sign it," he said.

Mateo said that Venceremos needed to provide resources for

workers to learn about their rights so they would understand how to respond when Tyson blamed them for accidents or fired them.

"Everyone here has a story," said Víctor.

Mateo added, "They have money for other people but not for the workers who process the chicken."

Víctor, upset, complained that Tyson's advertising was false. "Their banners and trucks show workers with masks that say 'Tyson, we are family.' They are brilliant when it comes to marketing." He described how, one day at work, a photographer asked workers to hug chicken nuggets for a new advertisement. His youngest child, Emerson, ran by, reminding Víctor of what he told his kids about chicken nuggets: "You love it, but you don't know what it is made of."

Sometimes, he told his kids how the sausage was made, describing the ground bones in the recipe. Víctor, supported by accounts of other workers, noted that the areas where the nuggets were made were often unclean. For example, when water gathered in pools, worms could often be found in the area. Alfredo told a story of worms falling from the ceiling. In response to the problem, someone at Tyson put down a piece of plastic. Víctor, laughing, said, "It's pure protein."

After breakfast on Saturday, April 2, the workers, their children, and local activists put on matching yellow JUSTICE FOR FARMWORKERS shirts and filed onto buses for the two-hour ride to Palm Beach. Víctor's youngest child, three years old, wore a t-shirt that fit him like a dress, and it dragged on the ground as he walked with a Spider-Man toy in his hands. In the early morning light, we drove past fields filled with workers. Mateo said of the CIW, "I have been thinking about everything I've seen. We need to use their model. As Magaly said—even fewer people buy tomatoes than chicken. Either they sink us, or we fight."

As everyone gathered in the parking lot, an agricultural worker stood up and said: "This campaign has reached many workers, and the only way is forward. They will be forced to listen to our demand for justice and sign the agreement. Heat and weariness don't affect us because justice is priceless. Today, we are joined by our friends, tireless fighters, many of whom have marched with us before. We will accompany each other forever because we believe in each other. Wendy's, get ready. We will surprise you."

On the two-hour bus ride from Immokalee to Palm Beach, Mateo, looking down, said, "I have three kids, and they wonder why I earn so little if I'm good at the work I do." He told several dairy workers seated nearby, also from Mexico, about a time he was injured: "One time, I slipped and fell and grabbed the conveyor belt with my hand. I cut myself deeply. That day, there was no nurse. I could see my bone." But his supervisor was only worried that he hadn't cleaned his blood off the production line because then the chicken on that line would have to be thrown away. Mateo remembered the incident because nobody asked him, "How are you?"

"This isn't going to be easy for us," Mateo said, talking about the work Venceremos wanted to do in Arkansas, "but Magaly wants to move forward." He thought agricultural workers in Florida might have had an easier battle than poultry workers in Arkansas, but he also knew they had been organizing for decades.

Several hundred people arrived for the march at manicured Bradley Park, which was located in a neighborhood of landscaped

mansions four miles from Mar-a-Lago. Florida agricultural workers, joined by poultry, dairy, and construction workers, held
tomato-shaped signs that read FIGHTING FOR FAIR FOOD
and RESPECT JUSTICE. They laughed, hugged, sang, and played
music. About half an hour before the march, the CIW set up
a stage in the park and presented a play to educate bystanders
about labor rights issues for tomato pickers. Lucas Benítez, the
cofounder of the CIW and a former farmworker, narrated the play
in Spanish with simultaneous English translation. The gathering
crowd witnessed tomato pickers handling cardboard vegetables
working under the protections of the Fair Food Program, while the
workers who weren't in the program suffered indignities, including
sexual harassment. The role of Peltz was played by Gerardo Reyes
Chávez, who helped launch the Fair Food Program, and CIW
members called him *El Flaco*. Wearing a white wig, he loomed
over a worker dressed up as the red-haired Wendy's mascot.

Reyes Chávez told me that Palm Beach had laws to prevent
protests, and the CIW had to sue the city in 2016 to gain the right
to assemble. The workers marched through the streets and stopped
at a high-end restaurant next to Peltz's office. Palm Beach residents
sitting in the street's cafés and restaurants were confronted, if only
for a moment, by the immigrant workers who provided their food.
"I think it was powerful to disturb them," said Magaly.

Upon returning to Arkansas, Víctor was fired. His supervisor
told him he had done his job wrong but refused to produce video
footage of his work area to prove it.

....

Back home in Green Forest, Quetzali barely opened the door and
only one of her eyes was visible. "They told me they didn't have

work for me because they only had work for people who could use two hands," she said of Tyson in early February 2023. "I'm depressed." She collapsed on the couch, crying.

Like many immigrant workers, she had flown home for Christmas to see her mother in Guatemala. Her mother, who was seventy-three, lived alone, had diabetes, and suffered from high blood pressure. To help pay the medical bills related to her carpal tunnel, Quetzali sold a small piece of land in Guatemala that she inherited from her dad.

When Quetzali returned to the Tyson plant in Green Forest on January 9, 2023, she was told to pick up chicken pieces from the floor, a job her supervisor said would be easier on her hands. But Quetzali was in pain and visited the nurse that day, who gave her bags of ice for her hands. The nurse told her she could do exercises independently to improve the condition of her hands, even though medical literature clearly states carpal tunnel syndrome can't be resolved without surgery unless it is diagnosed early and the symptoms aren't severe. Her supervisor, frustrated with her absence, said "there was no work for me because I didn't have two working hands." Quetzali was sent home and told to apply for disability.

Quetzali said, "They are punishing me, so I won't have money to continue. They are punishing me for opening my mouth." As for the pain, she managed it with pills and said, "I have to continue living while God gives me life."

Bobby continued to appear in Quetzali's dreams, and recently, Quetzali said, "He sat there"—pointing to the couch—"and crossed his hands and said, 'move forward or go to Guatemala.'"

She and Bobby rented the house, owned by a "White man"

in management at Tyson, for twenty-three years. "My husband taught me English," she said. "I received $4,500 when he died. Nothing. I paid for the sofas and a TV, and that was all, and the money was gone."

"I'm now bothering them, and they want to get rid of me. That's what they do with everyone. They did this to one person and gave them a bad record, and they can't get a job anywhere."

Tyson asked Quetzali to come to the plant for a meeting. A Tyson representative asked her the following questions: Are you a socialist? Do you have a boyfriend? How long have you lived with him? Quetzali said she was tempted to respond, "Are you a jealous man?" The representative wanted to know who was helping her financially. Quetzali said, "You know, at Tyson, if you get sick, you must keep working sick because you have to pay your bills. They know you don't have money, but they asked who helped me. I said my friend paid the rent."

She needed financial help and had consulted with Magaly, who suggested she post a GoFundMe campaign, which was how Tyson workers got support during critical periods while navigating the company bureaucracy. She didn't have the gas money to attend Venceremos meetings in Springdale.

Worried, Quetzali said, "People will come and damage my house," but, "at least, right now, there are no more armadillos under the house."

The eternal question asked by many outside the meatpacking industry is why workers like Quetzali don't find another job. Given that many workers are undocumented or don't speak English, their options for work, especially jobs that would allow them to send money to family members in their home countries, are few. Perhaps workers stay because they are haunted by memories of what their families endured in their home countries. They don't want to shut down the meatpacking industry—they want safe labor conditions.

In 2023, according to Arkansas Tyson workers, the company replaced much of the human resources department with the AskHR app. It relied on AI translation services to respond to workers in Marshallese, Karen, Thai, Vietnamese, Spanish, and dozens of other languages. Quetzali, who needed to use AskHR, said, "They have a policy now, and you must go online. They know many of us are illiterate, and even I don't know how to get into this app." Workers have said that the app makes it difficult to present safety and sexual harassment issues.

Quetzali calls her mom every day but doesn't tell her the extent of her condition. "When I am washing a dish, it falls. Even my telephone falls out of my hand, hits me in the face, and makes me bleed. It is part of my life. I'm already used to it. I don't have hope." Her evangelical mom said, "Daughter, you have to ask God for help."

Walking out of her house, I told Quetzali about my plans to travel to Mexico. "I'm going to visit Rosario and her mom," I said. Quetzali knew that my dream was to visit workers and their families in their home countries. She invited me to visit her mom in Guatemala that Christmas as well.

CONCLUSION: ROBOTS AND LAB-GROWN MEAT

In March of 2023, I drove several hours from Mexico City, which was my home from 2012 to 2020 when I worked as a journalist, to Querétaro. As I arrived at a house under construction, Rosario came out to the street to greet me in a bright red shirt that contrasted with her blond curls pressed tightly to her scalp as if wet. Her heart-shaped face was calm, and her green eyes looked transparent in the afternoon light. She said, "God bless you," as she ushered me through a white gate to a concrete patio filled with potted flowers and herbs. The house was calm and quiet—and mostly empty.

Her mother, Inés, seventy-six, sat in the bare kitchen of her son Thiago's house, a pile of chipilín, a medicinal plant with delicate yellow flowers from their native Guerrero, before her.

Inés's hands, a constellation of dark spots, were calloused, and her eyesight, she whispered, was leaving her. She wore a blue-and-white-patterned dress and a fleece cardigan as she separated the green leaves and yellow flowers from the stems and put the flowers in a blue bowl. Rosario spoke, her breath raspy as words escaped with effort. Pointing at her mom, she said she looked worn down because she had raised eight children alone.

"If I had stayed there longer, I wouldn't be alive to tell you this," said Rosario, sitting on an upturned plastic bucket beside her shrunken mother. She took the bus from Arkansas to Mexico in March 2023 to visit her mother. At the same time, she was waging a lawsuit to get disability payments from Tyson.

Rosario's family built the house over the years, buying concrete and tiles when they could afford materials.

Rosario's brother, Thiago, on a break from working on the house, was in the back bedroom watching TV with his kids. The floor in the kitchen was bare concrete, and a mattress wrapped in plastic sat in the middle of the room. The walls were recently painted white with a yellow stripe around the top. In the corner sat a stove, and next to it, a table covered with limes, chilies, bananas, and a large, clear plastic bag full of bread.

Rosario was nostalgic about her childhood despite the lack of money. Her earliest memories involved walking in the ocean tide and eating coconuts and mangos from the garden. But she never learned to swim and almost drowned in the ocean as a child, which resulted in a lifelong fear of water.

Her mom sold vegetables on the street, washed clothes, and did odd jobs. Her father, a Jehovah's Witness, spent his days preaching. "He lived with us, but he didn't even remember he had children," said Rosario. "My dad, rest in peace, spent all his time preaching." Rosario quit school at age twelve to help support her family.

Sitting in the kitchen with her mother in the late afternoon light, Rosario began to cough, apologizing. She couldn't breathe and got up to get some water out of a large plastic jug.

After the accident, Rosario felt her body was failing her—she was not the machine Tyson wished her to be: "They think human beings are robots, and they treat you like that. If you get sick, they look for excuses to fire you."

After the chemical accident, Rosario, despite health problems, needed to work at Tyson to support her family. One day, her daughter asked her, "Do you want to live, or do you want to die?" Rosario wanted to live but didn't want her daughter to lose the scholarship she had received from Tyson to attend the University of Arkansas.

As dusk settled, Rosario and Inés sat, talking as they prepared the chipilín to make tea. Before I left the house in Querétaro, Rosario stood up, opened the bread bag, and handed me two flat palm-sized rolls. As we walked outside, her mother picked a handful of flowering basil. She held a bunch up to my nose and placed it in my hand. Mother and daughter stood side by side as I drove away, their bodies fading into the night.

I texted Víctor that I wanted to visit his grandfather Jesús, who lived near Rosario's brother. In response, I received a photo of Víctor drinking tequila with Jesús at his house in Arkansas. At ninety-nine, Jesús had decided, on the spur of the moment, to take the bus from the small town of Hacienda la Caja to Springdale. Drinking tequila was a fine way to pass the time while waiting to find out when the lawsuit would become public.

....

By March 6, 2023, when the lawsuit was filed in Arkansas against Tyson Foods, thirty-four former employees and their family members had joined. For the first time, their names became public, a moment they had agonized over. Ultimately, they had all decided that they were more committed to justice than they were afraid of Tyson. Over sixty-nine pages, the lawsuit alleged that Tyson's negligence and disregard for its workers led to emotional distress, illness, and death.

The lawsuit summarized Angelina's case: "Plaintiff Pacheco also reasonably feared for the lives and safety of her family because they could contract COVID-19 from her husband's exposure at the Tyson facility. This reasonable fear caused Plaintiff Pacheco extreme emotional distress and mental anguish." Her son, Darío, also formed a part of the lawsuit, arguing that, because of "Tyson's near total disregard for safety," he was "only able to spend seven years of his life with his father." The lawsuit argued, "This reasonable fear caused Plaintiff Darío extreme emotional distress and mental anguish. Further, Tyson's acts and omissions led Plaintiff to believe that Tyson considered him to be less than human, expendable, and inferior. Overall, Tyson made Plaintiff feel as though his parents and his own life simply did not matter and that maximum production was more important than their health and safety." Darío became infected with COVID from his father and suffered from long-COVID symptoms.

The lawsuit lays out the mental, physical, emotional, and financial damage Tyson caused each family member of a worker who had died of COVID. The main arguments include the following: "Tyson's lack of concern for safety resulted in widespread infection of COVID."

The suit laid out similar arguments for each plaintiff: "Upon information and belief, Tyson lied to Plaintiff Pacheco about the number of Tyson employees that were contracting COVID-19 in an effort to maintain its rate of production at the Tyson facility." A disregard for COVID protocol at Tyson had resulted in high infection rates, which endangered family members.

In Rosario's case, the complaint detailed the impact of the chemical accident and how those injuries put her life at risk during the pandemic: "On June 22, 2011, Plaintiff Rosario suffered from a Tyson Plant accident where chemicals spilled near the job floor. Plaintiff Rosario was one of the last people to evacuate the building and, as a result, breathed in the toxic fumes from the spill. At the time, no supervisor was on site in order to assist with the evacuation. Plaintiff Rosario was admitted to the hospital overnight as a result of the spill. She was instructed by Tyson officials to return to work as soon as possible." The complaint argued that Rosario's respiratory condition and asthma made her "more susceptible to viruses like COVID-19."

The lawsuit framed Quetzali's case as follows: "Plaintiff Quetzali's husband contracted COVID-19 on or about June 16, 2020, as a result of working in a Tyson plant. Two days later, Plaintiff Quetzali's husband died as a result of COVID-19 on June 18, 2020. Witnessing her husband fear for his life as he went into work every day and suffer through COVID-19, which caused him extreme agony and eventually took his life, caused Plaintiff Quetzali extreme emotional distress and mental anguish. Plaintiff Quetzali was told by her supervisors not to talk about her husband's death, or she would be terminated. When her husband contracted COVID-19 and died, Plaintiff

Quetzali lost his love, comfort, and support. She further feels self-blame and shame from being a widow."

Víctor and Gloria, although they did not get COVID, formed a part of the suit. In the complaint, Víctor stated that Tyson lied about the number of Tyson employees who were contracting COVID. He used his paid time off (PTO) "to take two weeks off work, in the hope that Tyson would implement further health and safety protocols in response to COVID-19." Upon his return to work, no changes had been made. The suit described: "As a result of Tyson's total disregard for the safety of its employees, Plaintiff Víctor's mother, a Tyson employee at the Berry St. Plant, contracted COVID-19. After three days, Plaintiff Víctor's mother was forced to return to work or else receive an infraction. This caused Plaintiff Víctor further emotional distress and mental anguish."

In Gloria's case, the argument presented involved Tyson not enforcing social distancing, which caused her "extreme anxiety of contracting COVID-19 and spreading it to her family."

Mateo's complaint argued, "Through the COVID-19 pandemic, Plaintiff Mateo would report the need for protection to his supervisors and they would downplay the dangers of COVID-19. Tyson did not implement protocol to promote social distancing in his area. In fact, Tyson did not implement any safety protocol, in the wake of COVID-19, until it was pressured by the media to do so. Further, Tyson lied to Plaintiff Mateo about the total number of positive cases in the facility. Plaintiff Mateo was told by his manager that there was only one person sick in one department. Upon learning this, Plaintiff Mateo asked management if they were going to shut down the area to sanitize it, but they would only downplay the virus. Throughout the COVID-19 pandemic, Tyson management would blame the plant workers themselves if anyone would become ill, saying they went out partying on the weekends and brought any illness into the facility."

Margarita, like Víctor and Gloria, did not get COVID. The complaint focused on the impact of Margarita's work environment at the plant during the pandemic: "Plaintiff Margarita knew multiple coworkers, who she considered friends, who died as a result of COVID-19. Knowing that her coworkers died as a result of COVID-19, and that Tyson was doing nothing to prevent the spread of the virus at its facilities, caused Plaintiff Margarita extreme grief and emotional distress. Further, Tyson did not even recognize or announce the deaths of Plaintiff Margarita's coworkers." Margarita knew what it felt like to witness a disappearance that turned into a death.

The class action lawsuit could take years to unfold, and in the meantime, Tyson would try to solve their main problem—a lack of workers.

The company was constantly searching for someone or something to replace their most organized workers, like Quetzali, who needed the company to pay for carpal tunnel surgery in both hands. Or like Víctor and Gloria, who demanded safe working conditions and fair pay. Tyson executives had been thinking about how to replace workers for decades. In 2000, former Tyson Foods President Buddy Wray said, "Some of the things I see happening in robotics and I see happening in mechanization, and it will get to the point where we no longer have to have Hispanics." Wray mused that labor would soon cost $50 per hour. Wray wasn't an engineer but believed the company could invent a machine to replace the workers who deboned chicken.

Elvira, who worked at Tyson for six years before quitting, said, "They have to treat people right. We all have rights, and we aren't robots. They have us working as if we, the people, were robots." For Tyson, the answer to the labor issue wasn't to provide workers with safer conditions but to replace them. Wray envisioned a machine that would "take that chicken; you run it through some type of an x-ray that says ok, here is the bone structure of this bird that goes into the computer. The computer then operates this piece of robotics that takes the meat off the bone and knows exactly where the bone is to make the cut and all that stuff." The dream of replacing humans with machines was real, and Wray believed "we will find a way. American ingenuity will work if the government will let it."

Tyson treated workers like machines until they could develop the needed robots. Rosario, disabled from decades of work, said, "As long as you serve Tyson, you are a machine, and they don't bother you. But later, they threaten you when you don't serve them." Rosario admitted that she could never rest: "They convert us into robots, and we work in our sleep." And she wasn't the only one.

By April 2024, the court had closed the case made by the Tyson workers. In dry, legal language, the motion cited three main reasons for dismissing the case: first, that the Arkansas Workers' Compensation Commission has exclusive jurisdiction over claims arising out of injuries in the workplace, meaning the Arkansas court doesn't even have jurisdiction over those claims. Second, the workers' claims are barred by Arkansas's limited liability COVID immunity statute. Third, workers' claims are preempted by a federal law—the Poultry Products Inspection Act, which regulates poultry processing plants. This means that because the federal government can regulate the conduct of these plants, one can't bring a claim under state law trying to impose a different standard. The immigrant workers, who had hoped for justice, continued to cut chicken, but also to organize and share their stories. Their bodies knew a life of hard, dangerous work, but once they had imagined just labor conditions, they couldn't ask for anything less.

....

Changing the meatpacking industry requires reimagining the US food system, moving away from thoughtless consumption, and moving toward eating as a political act that acknowledges labor rights, animal rights, and the realities of climate change. As Alicia Kennedy argues in *No Meat Required*, "Eating ethically is an effort, a constant attempt to make choices regarding the consumption of food and goods that treads as lightly on the planet as possible while doing the least harm to humans and nonhuman animals. That means, of course, the most obvious thing: avoiding animal products. But it also means concern for the labor rights of farmworkers and the land rights of Indigenous and Black people, as well as a recognition of the necessity of access to fresh, local, culturally appropriate food and clean water for all the world's people. Not eating meat is to seek balance in ecology and the relationships between humans and nonhuman animals."

As food writer Ligaya Mishan argues, "Eating is intrinsically selfish. We eat to keep ourselves alive. And we often eat other living creatures, taking the lives of those we deem lesser (animals) in order to further our own. ... To take another angle, the perhaps undesirable truth is that food *should* be expensive, or at least more expensive than it is, given the toll agriculture

204 CONCLUSION: ROBOTS AND LAB-GROWN MEAT

takes on the environment and the labor required for planting and harvesting." As the era of endless and cheap meat consumption ends, politicians and consumers are reluctant to accept it.

While waiting for robotics to catch up with industry needs, Tyson Foods began to diversify, investing in meat products that were less labor intensive. In 2016 and 2017, Tyson Foods invested $34 million in the plant-based meat company, Beyond Meat. In 2022, Tyson announced that it would contribute to a $400 million investment in Upside Foods, a lab-grown meat company. Although many assumed that meatpacking companies would see lab-grown meat as a threat, the same profitable subsidies underpinning the meatpacking industry are flowing into lab-grown meat. The tech industry is selling lab-grown meat as if it were revolutionary, but it is simply an extension of the status quo in which the US continues to subsidize cheap and plentiful meat. Lab-grown meat is also a proprietary product, once again placing the food system in the hands of a few companies.

Lab-grown meat companies offer the illusion that nobody has to change: everyone can eat as much meat as they want, and nobody has to think about labor rights or climate change. Food writer Mishan notes, "The idea that not eating meat is a sacrifice (and possibly un-American) persists in the technological race to create nonmeat alternatives ... It's as if the only way to get people to stop eating beef is to trick them into thinking they're still eating it. Nothing has been lost, no sacrifice required."

Lab-grown meat companies offer Tyson a close look at their dream of a mostly robotic workforce run by a few highly trained employees. Upside Foods employees, for example, make an average salary of $86,552, and hourly workers earn $41.61/ hour. While the costs of biotech investment are incredibly high, lab-grown meat, given its novelty and promise, is experiencing massive investment from the US government and private investors.

Like the meatpacking industry, lab-grown meat would have to be heavily subsidized by the government to be affordable to most consumers. The US government would continue to fund Big Ag companies and the endless consumption of meat in any form. As Kennedy argues in No Meat Required, "The animals might be absent in this idea of the future, industrial animal agriculture decimated by the dominance of tech burgers and lab meat, but meat as an idea will remain and it will continue to be the dominant food. There's been so much work done to change that idea, yet capital is leading us right back."

The lab-grown meat industry has sold itself as "the future of food," but it should be called the future of meat. Lab-cultured meat is an extension of the current system in which resources are invested in existing Big Ag companies rather than in solutions that recognize the future of food doesn't involve industrially produced meat. Kennedy wrote of lab-grown meat and tech burgers: "What they represent is a continuation of meat-as-symbol that I find rather troubling, because I personally want to see a radical reimagining of how we eat, how we use land, and how we think about our food." Rather than radically reimagine what our food system could look like and how we could care for workers and the environment, we find the same companies and political powers investing their money, energy, and time in producing meat.

Some companies first extract cells from a living animal's muscle and skin tissue and collect fetal bovine serum (FBS) from the unborn fetuses of slaughtered cows to create lab-grown meat. Cell-cultured meat is grown in a lab; the resulting product is a single-cell slurry, a mix of 30 percent animal cells and 70 percent water. The slurry can make ground meat products such as burgers and nuggets. The long-term health consequences of eating lab-cultivated meat remain unknown.

Companies making lab-cultured meat, like meatpacking companies, require government subsidization. Both the meatpacking industry and lab-cultured meat exert a high environmental cost. While it is known that the meatpacking industry contributes to climate change by raising and killing animals, early studies suggest that lab-grown meat's carbon footprint is worse than retail beef. Kennedy says, "Meat maintains its central role because people can't imagine another way forward."

....

Víctor had read that Tyson was investing in lab-grown meat. "I don't know if it will work for them. People could try their synthetic meat, but it probably doesn't have the same taste," said Víctor, sitting in a folding chair in his garage, his tools spread around him as he worked on an old truck. Even after he was fired from Tyson, at night he dreamed he was deboning chickens and felt his hands spring into action. Sitting in the garage, his hands jumped into the air, gripping an imaginary knife and plunging it with the force necessary to cut through flesh and bone. "It takes me three to five seconds to cut each set of chicken wings," he said. His hands continued to move, darting with precision from one point in the air to another, a circuit that his body had memorized.

Reflecting on the future of Tyson, Víctor said, "They don't want people anymore. They don't need them. In their plans for the future, workers don't exist. They want to produce meat without workers. It is a science fiction future where they don't care about workers and don't need them."

Víctor, afraid of losing his immigration status, has never returned to Mexico. His grandfather Jesús, who became a centenarian in 2023, took the bus to Arkansas each year to visit. Jesús wore wide-brimmed straw hats, shirts with pearl buttons and gold embroidery, and handmade leather belts with ornate buckles. His face was long and lined, his hands worn but nimble. Jesús remembered Víctor as a mischievous child and described his sadness when the family migrated to the US. "They told me they would return soon," Jesús said, sighing, "but they didn't." Víctor and Jesús drank tequila while exchanging stories about family in Mexico, farming, and work. Víctor asked Jesús, "What advice would you give someone who wants to reach your age?" Jesús responded, "Behave, treat yourself well, and live right." Jokingly, to test Jesús's memory, Víctor asked him to name his eleven children. "Manuel died, and then John," Jesús remembered, before naming the rest. Sometimes, Jesús stayed in Arkansas for a month or more in the summer, enough time to witness the squash and tomato plants in his grandchildren's gardens bearing fruit.

After getting fired from Tyson, Víctor got a job at a cookie factory. He still attends Venceremos meetings and keeps in touch with Tyson workers to document conditions at the plants. "I learned that we can achieve things by working together," he told me. "As workers, we have many rights we don't know about."

At the cookie factory, Víctor makes $16/hour, $5 less per hour than at Tyson. He said, "The work is different, but the labor conditions are better. I like making cookies." The managers at the cookie factory listen to him, and never yell at him, insult him, or follow him to the bathroom. And if he needs permission to go to the doctor or pick up his kids from school, he receives it, unlike at Tyson, where he had to fight for similar requests.

When I visited him recently he said, "Next time you visit, buy half a dozen whole chickens. We'll put them on cones in the yard, and I'll show you how to debone them," because the effects of the repetitive motion labor lived on in his body, his memory, and his dreams. "We are in the mouth of the wolf," he said, reflecting on the fight that workers continued to wage for safe labor conditions, "To win, we have to weaken them. *Sí, se puede*. Yes, we can do it."

ACKNOWLEDGMENTS

The idea for this book was born in 2013 when my mom, Louise Halsey, volunteered with the immigrant Karen community in Clarksville, Arkansas. The Karen were nearly 8,600 miles from their home in Myanmar working in rural Arkansas in the meatpacking industry. My mom helped Nok, the daughter of one family, get the necessary documents to enroll in high school. In a letter to me, my mom wrote, "I am working on getting my new Burmese daughters acclimated to life in Clarksville. The seventeen-year-old is going to start tenth grade, and she has almost no English skills. I asked about her clothing situation. She went to Walmart (where else is there?), and things were too big, too long, and not colors she liked. She and her sister wear wrapped skirts, loose tops, and flip-flops, but winter will come, and they will need real clothes. I think the one attending high school needs to have the trappings of belonging as much as possible." In another letter, my mom wrote, "The extended family bought a house, moved in, and were doing well with most members working at Tyson, a fate I hoped to help my high schooler avoid." Reading her letter, I knew I wanted to write about the meatpacking industry's reliance on immigrants and refugees—and ultimately understand the lives of those immigrants and refugees living in far-flung, rural towns.

As a freelance writer, I tried for almost a decade to write this story, but didn't get a grant to support the work until 2020. Although the idea for the book evolved, it is rooted in the letters my mom wrote me about the Karen as they tried to make a life in Arkansas. In the early months of the pandemic in 2020, I drove across the state, spending hours on the road with photographer Liz Sanders, to visit Tyson workers at their homes. As meatpacking workers became infected with and died of Covid, I feared that I could never do them justice. At that time, I had run out of money and moved into my parents' house in the Ozarks. I spent much of 2020 in a state of insomnia as I witnessed the families of meatpacking workers struggle with medical and funeral bills. When I met my agent, Kirsty McLachlan, in 2020, she believed in my vision at a time when I was tired, scared, broke, and facing mounting obstacles to my investigative work. Her kindness and thoughtfulness have gotten me through the past years of interviews. Even though McLachlan lives in London and we have never met in person, she saw me for the writer I was and wanted to be, and forever changed my life.

To my brilliant and poetic editor, Alessandra Bastagli, thank you for your commitment to this book and your patience when I felt weary and unable to write. When I disappeared for months at a time and was late to turn in the manuscript (and sure that it was a mess), your wisdom and encouragement got me into a better mental space. Your faith in me and in the importance of this story carried me to the finish line. Thank you to Joanna Pinsker, Abby Mohr, Sonja Singleton, Paige Lytle, and the One Signal team.

This book exists because of the wild bravery and generosity of the workers who shared their lives with me. Your tenacity and humor gave me the courage to keep investigating even when this work seemed impossible. My greatest thanks to everyone who opened their homes to me, sharing moments of love, loss, and grief. To labor organizer Magaly Licolli, the Director of Venceremos, thank you for your fierce sense of justice and commitment to meatpacking workers.

In the early stages of working on this book, I called Yuri Herrera while parked on the side of a rural highway sobbing, overwhelmed by the deaths of meatpacking workers, worried that I would not be able to write this book. He said, "Create an obsessive space. Do not doubt your work—you have something precious here." When I was full of doubt about the book, C. E. Morgan wrote me, "I've sort of never accepted 'no' for an answer, and I've just plowed ahead." My greatest thanks to poet Nikky Finney, my professor at Berea College, who taught me that "so much of the world needs the muscle found in true words. Please keep sending what your head and your belly make as one loaf." And to writer Elena Poniatowska, who, when I interviewed her at ninety-one, told me she wanted to write until her last day. Me too, Elena.

To the residencies that supported me while I wrote this book, thank you for providing me the necessary balance of silence, peace, and community to write my manuscript: I was a resident at Yaddo, at Mesa Refuge, where I was a Michael Pollan Journalism Fellow, at Jentel Artist Residency, and at the Logan Nonfiction Program. Thank you to the National Geographic Society, the Pulitzer Center, and the Economic Hardship Reporting Project for providing the funding to begin this project. And what a tremendous honor to win the 2024 J. Anthony Lukas Work-in-Progress Award for this book.

I would like to thank the Reporters Committee for Freedom of the Press and ProJourn, the Protecting Journalists Pro Bono Program, specifically Christina Piaia for connecting me with the Cornell Law School First Amendment Clinic. I am indebted to the talented team at Cornell for providing a legal review of my manuscript, including Dr. Mark Jackson, the Director of the First Amendment Clinic, Dr. Heather Murray, the Managing Attorney of the Local Journalism Project, and law students Dominic Muscarella and Iain Patrick Smith.

Thank you to Jasper Burroughs, a law student at UC Irvine who received class credit for providing a legal perspective on the developing class action lawsuit in my book. My deepest gratitude to Joshua Sharpe and Bronwen Dickey who, in addition to providing early and moving feedback on the manuscript, saw me through the period of book writing where I was crying on the floor and deeply in despair about finishing. For me, writing is intimately tied to photography. For this book, I worked with photographers Liz Sanders, Jacky Muniello, and John Stanmeyer to capture the daily life of workers in ways poetic and moving. I am indebted to editors Lee van der Voo, Matt Seaton, and Mike

Dang, who supported this project in its early stages when meat-packing workers were becoming infected with Covid in great numbers—your belief in this work allowed me to imagine that it could be a book. A very special thank-you to Mark Bowden, the author of *Black Hawk Down*, for the early feedback he provided on my manuscript.

To my dear writer, photographer, artist, and filmmaker friends who supported me during this process, thank you for carrying me through the difficult moments. To Jill Damatac, who I met in a writing class at Berea College when she was navigating life as an undocumented person, it is true serendipity that two decades later we are sisters in book writing and share the same wonderful editor. And to Fernanda Santos, Billy Higgins, Erica Chenoweth, Sloane Crosley, Jaime Quatro, Nicole Christian, Alejandra Oliva, Julie Schwietert Collazo, Brooke Bierhaus Sutton, Alicia Kennedy, Anna Sulan Masing, Suzan Meryem Rosita, Alfredo Corchado, Lauren Bohn, Verónica Cárdenas, Griselda San Martín, Sameer Ashar, Marielena Hincapié, Sari Botton, Diana Goetsch, Catalina Gómez, Andrea Pitzer, Yaffa Fredrick, Maya Goded, Cassy Dorff, Sari Botton, Drea Cofield, Carol Lipnik, Dashaun Washington, Dustin Metz, Blair Braverman, Yaffa Fredrick, Liu Xiaodong, Kathleen Flynn, Julianne Chandler, Bruna Dantas Lobato, Cecily Raynor, Mónica Vallin, Justin Tyler Bryant, Kensuke Yamada, Eyal Press, Lisa Pruitt, and Christopher Leonard. To the summer swim team at the Logan Nonfiction Program, Karen Pinchin and Max Duncan, how fun it was to swim across the lake each morning with you.

To Fred de Rosset and Margarita Graetzer, my Spanish professors at Berea College, my work is grounded in what I learned from you about language, translation, justice, and faith.

To Lucy Ynosencio, Lea Jacuzzi, and Rachel Driver Speckan, who I have known since the day I was born at home in Oark, Arkansas, I am thankful that we still laugh with the same wild abandon that we did as girls. To Emily Burroughs Strobo and Annie Laurie Pettit Yeiser, who sent me a video message from Roxane Gay for my birthday, thank you for your love and support of my writerly ambitions. And to Thuytien Truong, my best friend since Berea College, I treasure our daily video chats when you call me from Thailand to discuss what you are eating for breakfast and the meaning of life. To my parents, Louise Halsey and Stephen Driver, who saw me through COVID, insomnia, and the fear and financial strain that marked my journey to write this book. A potter and a weaver, you made art your way of life—I love you.

NOTES

AUTHOR'S NOTE ON MORAL BEAUTY

XII *In The Jungle* Upton Sinclair, *The Jungle* (Penguin Classics, 1985).

XIII *companies controlled the market* Alison Moodie, "Fowl Play: The Chicken Farmers Being Bullied by Big Poultry," *Guardian*, April 22, 2017. https://www.theguardian.com/sustainable -business/2017/apr/22/chicken-farmers-big-poultry-rules

XIII *impact of COVID on the meatpacking industry* Alice Driver, "Their Lives on the Line," *New York Review of Books*, April 27, 2021. https://www.nybooks.com/online/2021/04/27/their-lives -on-the-line/

XV *class action lawsuit against Tyson Foods* Dee-Ann Durbin, "Tyson Workers Sue Company over Lack of COVID Protections During Early Days of the Pandemic," *Fortune*, March 7, 2023. https://fortune.com/2023/03/07/tyson -workers-sue-company-over-lack-covid-protections-during -early-days-pandemic/

XV *I am moved to do this work by what author C. E. Morgan* I met C. E. Morgan while studying English at Berea College in rural Kentucky. Berea, founded in 1855 to educate freed slaves and students with limited economic resources, is a college rooted in the tradition of social justice.

XVI *love is not a feeling but an action* Anthony Domestico, "An Interview with C.E. Morgan, *"Commonweal*, May 19, 2016. https://www.commonwealmagazine.org/i-want-soul

CHAPTER 1: WORKING IN THEIR SLEEP

7 *just as she did at the poultry processing plant* Alice Driver, "Working in Their Sleep," *New York Review of Books*, December 23, 2022. https://www.nybooks.com/online/2022/12/23/working-in-their-sleep/

9 *pork sold in America* Dominick Reuter, "Meet the Billionaire Family Behind Tyson Foods, the Beef, Pork, and Chicken Juggernaut Whose Heir Apparent Has Battled Legal Troubles," *Business Insider*, August 8, 2023. https://www.businessinsider.com/who-owns-tyson-foods-history-2023-5

9 *about 18 percent of the meatpacking company's annual sales* Lisa Held, "Walmart's 'Regenerative Foodscape,'" *Civil Eats*, November 1, 2023. https://civileats.com/2023/11/01/walmarts-regenerative-foodscape/

9 *that wield extraordinary influence* Rebecca Boehm, "Tyson Spells Trouble for Arkansas: Its Near-Monopoly on Chicken Threatens Farmers, Workers, and Communities," *Union of Concerned Scientists*, August 11, 2021. https://www.ucsusa.org/resources/tyson-spells-trouble#read-online-content

9 *and 85 percent of the beef market* The White House, "Fact Sheet: The Biden-Harris Action Plan for a Fairer, More Competitive, and More Resilient Meat and Poultry Supply Chain," The White House, January 03, 2022. https://www.whitehouse.gov/briefing-room/statements-releases/2022/01/03/fact-sheet-the-biden-harris-action-plan-for-a-fairer-more-competitive-and-more-resilient-meat-and-poultry-supply-chain/

9 *and relax industry oversight* Claire Kelloway, "How Biden Can Rein in the Big Meat Monopoly," *Vox*, February 24, 2021. https://www.vox.com/future-perfect/22298043/meat-antitrust-biden-vilsack

10 *even as profits soared* The Northwest Arkansas Workers' Justice Center, "Wages and Working Conditions in Arkansas Poultry Plants," February 1, 2016. https://www.uusc.org/sites/default

/files/wages_and_working_conditions_in_arkansas_poultry
_plants.pdf

10 *lower prices for consumers, either* Boehm, "Tyson Spells
Trouble."

10 *a doctor is not approved* Debbie Berkowitz and Patrick Dixon,
"An Average of 27 Workers a Day Suffer Amputation or
Hospitalization According to New OSHA Data from 29 States,"
Economic Policy Institute, March 30, 2023. https://www.epi
.org/blog/an-average-of-27-workers-a-day-suffer-amputation-or
-hospitalization-according-to-new-osha-data-from-29-st
ates-meat-and-poultry-companies-remain-among-the-most
-dangerous/

10 *50 percent of the meatpacking workforce* Brent Orrell,
"Hypocrisy Strikes: 'Essential Workers' and the Meat Packing
Industry," American Enterprise Institute, April 29, 2020. https://
www.aei.org/opportunity-social-mobility/hypocrisy-strikes
-essential-workers-and-the-meat-packing-industry/

10 *Pacific Islanders employed* Angela Stuesse and Nathan T. Dollar,
"Who Are America's Meat and Poultry Workers?" Economic
Policy Institute, September 24, 2020. https://www.epi.org/blog
/meat-and-poultry-worker-demographics/

10 *suffering amputation or hospitalization* Berkowitz and Dixon,
"An Average of 27 Workers a Day."

10 *almost 500,000 workers nationwide* Debbie Berkowitz, Anna D.
Goff, Kathleen Marie Fagan, and Monica L. Gerrek, "Do Clinics
in Meat and Poultry Plants Endanger Workers?," *AMA Journal
of Ethics*, April 2023. https://journalofethics.ama-assn.org
/article/do-clinics-meat-and-poultry-plants-endanger-workers
/2023-04

11 *are 29.5 percent Hispanic and 26.8 percent Black* Chris
Casey, "Tyson to Conduct Racial Equity Audit," *Food Drive*,
December 14, 2021. https://www.fooddive.com/news/tyson-to
-conduct-racial-equity-audit/611468/

11 *Tennessee, Texas, and Virginia* David Barboza, "Tyson Foods
Indicted in Plan to Smuggle Illegal Workers," *New York
Times*, December 20, 2001. https://www.nytimes.com/2001
/12/20/us/tyson-foods-indicted-in-plan-to-smuggle-illegal
-workers.html

11 *coroner ruled it a suicide* Associated Press, "Suicide in Tyson Foods Case," *New York Times*, April 20, 2002. https://www .nytimes.com/2002/04/20/us/national-briefing-south-tennessee -suicide-in-tyson-foods-case.html

12 *"how he accomplishes the tasks"* Author Christopher Leonard shared recordings of these internal interviews with me. He obtained the recordings after his book about Tyson Foods, *The Meat Racket*, was published in 2014. The recordings are from a series of video interviews with Leland Tollett, the chief executive officer at Tyson Foods from 1991 to 1998, and Donald "Buddy" Wray, who served as president of the company from 1991 to 2000. The videos were made for internal use at Tyson Foods.

12 *helping them obtain counterfeit work documents* David Barboza, "Chicken Well Simmered in a Political Stew; Tyson Fosters Ties to Officials but Is Unable to Avoid Scrutiny," *New York Times*, January 1, 2002. https://www.nytimes.com/2002/01/01 /business/chicken-well-simmered-political-stew-tyson-fosters -ties-officials-but-unable.html

12 *acquitted Tyson and three managers of smuggling* Sherri Day, "Jury Clears Tyson Foods in Use of Illegal Immigrants," *New York Times*, March 27, 2003. https://www.nytimes.com/2003 /03/27/us/jury-clears-tyson-foods-in-use-of-illegal-immigrants .html

12 *profit from hiring undocumented workers* Stephen Groves and Sophia Tareen, "U.S. Meatpacking Industry Relies on Immigrant Workers. But a Labor Shortage Looms," *Los Angeles Times*, May 26, 2020. https://www.latimes.com/food/story/2020-05-26 /meatpacking-industry-immigrant-undocumented-workers

12 *lobbying the US government* Isaiah Poritz, "Biden Sets Sights on the Meat Processing Industry While Lobbying Soars," *Open Secrets*, September 13, 2021. https://www.opensecrets.org/news /2021/09/biden-sets-sights-on-the-meat-processing-industry -while-lobbying-soars/#:~:text=Although%20overall%20 expenditures%20on%20lobbying,and%20%241.7%20 million%20in%202016

12 *spent $25 million to block climate policies* Sigal Samuel, "It's Not Just Big Oil. Big Meat Also Spends Millions to Crush Good Climate Policy," *Vox*, April 13, 2021. https://www.vox.com

/future-perfect/22379909/big-meat-companies-spend-millions
-lobbying-climate

12 *shield concentrated animal feeding operations from EPA fines*
Matt McConnell, "When We're Dead and Buried, Our Bones Will
Keep Hurting," Human Rights Watch, September 4, 2019. https://
www.hrw.org/report/2019/09/04/when-were-dead-and-buried
-our-bones-will-keep-hurting/workers-rights-under-threat

12 *chance of being inspected by the Occupational Safety and Health
Administration* Dave Dickey, "Opinion: Big Meat Lobbyists Are
Bullying Lawmakers into Submission," *Investigate Midwest*,
June 1, 2023. https://investigatemidwest.org/2023/06/01/big
-meat-lobbyists-are-bullying-lawmakers-into-submission/

13 *"understand that we're trying to be fair"* Author Christopher
Leonard shared recordings of these internal interviews with me.
He obtained the recordings after his book about Tyson Foods,
The Meat Racket, was published in 2014. The recordings are
from a series of video interviews with Leland Tollett, the chief
executive officer at Tyson Foods from 1991 to 1998, and Donald
"Buddy" Wray, who served as president of the company from
1991 to 2000. The videos were made for internal use at Tyson
Foods.

13 *"I don't see that changing"* Author Christopher Leonard shared
recordings of these internal interviews with me. He obtained the
recordings after his book about Tyson Foods, *The Meat Racket*,
was published in 2014. The recordings are from a series of video
interviews with Leland Tollett, the chief executive officer at
Tyson Foods from 1991 to 1998, and Donald "Buddy" Wray,
who served as president of the company from 1991 to 2000. The
videos were made for internal use at Tyson Foods.

13 *Freedom from Addiction through Christ* Amy Julia Harris and
Shoshana Walter, "These Are the Rehabs That Make People
Work in Chicken Plants," *Reveal*, October 5, 2017. https://
revealnews.org/blog/these-are-the-rehabs-that-make-people
-work-in-chicken-plants/

14 *a pipeline of low-paid workers* The Tyson Foods webpage
states, "We strive to operate with integrity and trust in all we
do. We strive to honor God and be respectful of each other, our
customers, and other stakeholders."

14 *like Cassady Broiler Company and Cobb-Vantress* Christopher
    Leonard, *The Meat Racket* (Simon and Schuster, 2014), 108.

14 *when the shifts change at some Tyson plants in Arkansas*
    Hannah Dreier, "Tyson and Perdue Are Facing Child Labor
    Investigations," *New York Times*, September 23, 2023. https://
    www.nytimes.com/2023/09/23/us/tyson-perdue-child-labor.html

15 *$30 billion annually in federal funding to agribusiness* Chris
    Edwards, "Cutting Federal Farm Subsidies," CATO Institute,
    August 31, 2023. https://www.cato.org/briefing-paper/cutting
    -federal-farm-subsidies

16 *blood of animals have long been seen in many cultures* Eyal Press,
    "Shadow People," in *Dirty Work: Essential Jobs and the Hidden
    Toll of Inequality in America* (Farrar, Straus and Giroux, 2021),
    164.

CHAPTER 2: SAFE WORK

19 *"Safe work is the only work at Tyson"* Mary Hennigan, Abby
    Zimmardi, and Rachel Sanchez-Smith, "At Least 9,000 Workers
    Caught COVID-19 as Pandemic Overwhelmed Regulators,
    Companies," Howard Center for Investigative Journalism,
    May 12, 2021. https://cnsmaryland.org/2021/05/12/at-least
    -9000-arkansas-workers-caught-covid-19-as-pandemic
    -overwhelmed-regulators-companies/

19 *inside the expansive fenced property* Staff, "Tyson Foods
    Considers New Plant in Arkansas," *Meat + Poultry*, April 14,
    2016. https://www.meatpoultry.com/articles/14147-tyson-foods
    -considers-new-plant-in-arkansas#:~:text=The%20new%20
    plant%20is%20valued,%2Dft

19 *framed this as an effort to protect trade secrets* Leighton
    Akio Woodhouse, "Charged with the Crime of Filming a
    Slaughterhouse," *Nation*, July 31, 2013. https://www.thenation
    .com/article/archive/charged-crime-filming-slaughterhouse/

19 *audio or video inside company installations* Barbara Grzincic,
    "8th Circuit Revives Challenge to Arkansas Ag-Gag Law,"
    Reuters, August 10, 2021. https://www.reuters.com/legal
    /litigation/8th-circuit-revives-challenge-arkansas-ag-gag
    -law-2021-08-10/#:~:text=(Reuters)%20%2D%20A%20

divided%20federal,surreptitiously%20records%20
operations%20and%20shares

20 *health and safety in the meatpacking industry* Rebecca Boehm,
"Tyson Spells Trouble for Arkansas: Its Near-Monopoly on
Chicken Threatens Farmers, Workers, and Communities," Union
of Concerned Scientists, August 11, 2021. https://www.ucsusa
.org/resources/tyson-spells-trouble#read-online-content

20 *nonslip soles, hearing protection, and goggles* "Personal
Protective Equipment," Occupational Safety and Health
Administration. https://www.osha.gov/personal-protective
-equipment

20 *evisceration, and carcass-chilling areas* "Fully-Cooked Food
Production Plant in Virginia to Drive Business Growth," Tyson
Foods, November 29, 2023. https://www.tysonfoods.com
/news/news-releases/2023/11/tyson-foods-opens-innovative
-new-fully-cooked-food-production-plant#:~:text=The%20
325%2C000%2Dsquare%2Dfoot%20facility,both%20in%20
retail%20and%20foodservice

20 *can cause hearing damage* Grace Hatfield, "Back to Basics:
Meatpacking Hazards," *EHS Daily Advisor*, September 26,
2022. https://ehsdailyadvisor.blr.com/2022/09/back-to-basics
-meatpacking-hazards/

21 *typically for twelve-hour shifts* Hannah Dreier, "The Kids on the
Night Shift," *New York Times Magazine*, September 18, 2023.
https://www.nytimes.com/2023/09/18/magazine/child-labor
-dangerous-jobs.html

21 *independent farmers contracted by Tyson* "Feeding the World
with America's Poultry Farmers," Tyson Foods. https://www
.tysonfoods.com/who-we-are/our-partners/farmers/contract
-poultry-farming

21 *the poultry processing facility they supply* Boehm, "Tyson Spells
Trouble for Arkansas."

22 *had been working sixteen-hour days* Daniel Caruth, "Poultry
Worker Advocates Protest Tyson over Child Labor Allegations,"
KUAF NPR affiliate, October 31, 2023. https://www.kuaf.com
/show/ozarks-at-large/2023-10-31/poultry-worker-advocates
-protest-tyson-over-child-labor-allegations

23 *where there is less oversight* "Exposed: Tyson Workers Torturing

Birds, Urinating on Slaughter Line," PETA. https://support.peta
.org/page/1843/action/1

23 *reflected in a pool of blood* Michael Grabell, "Exploitation and
Abuse at the Chicken Plant," *New Yorker,* May 1, 2017. https://
www.newyorker.com/magazine/2017/05/08/exploitation-and
-abuse-at-the-chicken-plant

23 *near its headquarters in Springdale* Nathan Owens, "Tyson
Opens New Robotics Center," *Arkansas Democrat Gazette,*
August 9, 2019. https://www.arkansasonline.com/news/2019
/aug/09/tyson-opens-new-robotics-center-downtow/

23 *a "captive market" for gizzard burgers* Douglas Frantz, "How
Tyson Became the Chicken King," *New York Times,* August 28,
1994. https://www.nytimes.com/1994/08/28/business/how
-tyson-became-the-chicken-king.html

27 *reach their daily production quotas* Elizabeth Chuck, "Poultry
Workers, Denied Bathroom Breaks, Wear Diapers: Oxfam
Report," NBC News, May 12, 2016. https://www.nbcnews.com
/business/business-news/poultry-workers-denied-bathroom
-breaks-wear-diapers-oxfam-report-n572806

27 *one thirty-minute unpaid break* Huiqi Xu, Maureen Strode,
and Andrew Withers, "Poultry Processing Workers Face Injuries
in Wisconsin, Nationwide," Midwest Center for Investigative
Reporting, July 15, 2018. https://captimes.com/news/local
/govt-and-politics/poultry-processing-workers-face-injuries
-in-wisconsin-nationwide/article_4c3519f0-0e54-546a
-9258-f7d3b63af0ba.html#:~:text=At%20Tyson%2C%20
Burleson%20said%20team,of%20more%20than%2020%20
minutes

28 *go to the bathroom more than once* Chuck, "Poultry Workers,
Denied Bathroom Breaks."

29 *"Like the decapitation"* Kate Ng, "Worker Decapitated in
Industrial Accident at Alabama Chicken Plant," *Independent,*
March 6, 2020. https://www.independent.co.uk/news/world
/americas/alabama-carlos-lynn-decapitated-chicken-processing
-plant-a9381426.html

29 *a Black man from Alabama* Carlos Robinson, "Worker
Decapitated in Industrial Accident at Alabama Chicken Plant,"
AL.com, March 4, 2020. https://www.al.com/news/2020/03

/worker-decapitated-in-industrial-accident-at-alabama-chicken
-plant.html

32 *the continued violation of labor rights* Noam Scheiber, "OSHA
Criticized for Lax Regulation of Meatpacking in Pandemic,"
New York Times, October 22, 2020. https://www.nytimes
.com/2020/10/22/business/economy/osha-coronavirus-meat
.html#:~:text=The%20JBS%20case%20reflects%20a,a%20
total%20of%20less%20than

32 *1 percent of the companies it regulated* Mark Gruenberg,
"OSHA Inspects Less Than One-Half of 1% of Firms Yearly,"
People's World, May 26, 2022.

35 *Immigration and Reform Control Act* Michael Grabell,
"Exploitation and Abuse at the Chicken Plant," *New Yorker*,
May 1, 2017. https://www.newyorker.com/magazine/2017/05
/08/exploitation-and-abuse-at-the-chicken-plant

CHAPTER 3: THE CHICKEN NUGGETS RECIPE

42 *with industrial volumes of chicken* A Tyson worker recorded
videos while at work and shared them with me. These
descriptions are based on his videos.

43 *transport chickens to market* Christopher Leonard, *The Meat
Racket* (Simon and Schuster, 2014).

43 *"to have a bad time"* Globe Newswire, "Don Tyson, Former
Tyson Foods Chairman and CEO, Passes Away, NBC News,
January 6, 2011. https://www.nbcnews.com/id/wbna40947562

43 *campaigns across the state* Michael Kelly, "The President's Past,"
New York Times, July 31, 1994. https://www.nytimes.com/1994
/07/31/magazine/the-president-s-past.html

44 *later transferred to the University of Arkansas* Paul Gatling,
"Buddy Wray Remembered," *TP&B*, February 1, 2016. https://
talkbusiness.net/2016/02/buddy-wray-remembered/

44 *as sharing the same values* From the interviews conducted
in 2000 with Leland Tollett and Buddy Wray that journalist
Christopher Leonard shared with me.

44 *what kind of home life they had* From the interview conducted
in 2000 with Buddy Wray that journalist Christopher Leonard
shared with me.

44 *continue to grow the company* Robert D. McFadden, "Donald J. Tyson, Food Tycoon, Is Dead at 80," *New York Times*, January 6, 2011. https://www.nytimes.com/2011/01/07/business /07tyson.html

45 *significantly better profit margins* T. Rees Shapiro, "Don Tyson, Politically Connected 'Chicken King' of Arkansas, Dies at 80," *Washington Post*, February 25, 2011. https:// www.washingtonpost.com/obituaries/don_tyson_politically _connected_chicken_king_of_arkansas_dies_at_80/2011/01/06 /ABCU5jD_story.html

45 *"a business cowboy that just takes the shots"* From the interview conducted in 2000 with Leland Tollett that journalist Christopher Leonard shared with me.

45 *have shaped politics and policies in the state and nation* Olivia Paschal, "The Modern-Day Company Towns of Arkansas," *American Prospect*, August 1, 2022. https://prospect.org/power /modern-day-company-towns-of-arkansas/

45 *infant and maternal mortality rates* Oriana González, "Maternal Deaths Have Spiked in Arkansas in the Last 20 Years," *Axios*, July 11, 2023. https://www.axios.com/local/nw -arkansas/2023/07/11/arkansas-maternal-death-rate-spikes

45 *University of Arkansas School of Law in Fayetteville* Sara Fritz, "Clinton Ties to Tyson Scion Still Drawing Critics' Fire," *Los Angeles Times*, June 12, 1994. https://www.latimes.com /archives/la-xpm-1994-06-12-mn-3410-story.html

45 *enjoying the company of young women* McFadden, "Donald J. Tyson, Food Tycoon."

46 *his meetings with Wall Street analysts* McFadden, "Donald J. Tyson, Food Tycoon."

46 *Cabo San Lucas, Mexico* United States District Court for the District of Columbia, Securities Exchange Commission, Plaintiff v. Tyson Foods, Inc. and Donald Tyson. https://www.sec.gov /files/litigation/complaints/comp19208.pdf

46 *would last for decades* David Maraniss and Michael Weisskopf, "In Arkansas, the Game Is Chicken," *Washington Post*, March 22, 1992. https://www.washingtonpost.com/archive/politics /1992/03/22/in-arkansas-the-game-is-chicken/6244e0fa-5416 -4a6a-bae8-a229b854ed98/

46 *"he was impressive"* Kelly, "The President's Past."

46 *meatpacking industry regulations* Chris Kromm, "Inside the Tyson Foods Empire," *Facing South*, May 2, 2005. https://www.facingsouth.org/2005/05/inside-the-tyson-foods-empire.html

46 *contributed to Tyson's growth* Fritz, "Clinton Ties to Tyson Scion."

46 *the founder of Walmart* McFadden, "Donald J. Tyson, Food Tycoon."

46 *Arkansas is small and insulated* Jeff Garth, "The 1992 Campaign: Candidate's Record; Policies Under Clinton Are a Boon to Industry," *New York Times*, April 2, 1992. https://www.nytimes.com/1992/04/02/us/1992-campaign-candidate-s-record-policies-under-clinton-are-boon-industry.html

46 *friendship and financial dealings* Fritz, "Clinton Ties to Tyson Scion."

47 *nearly $100,000 in ten months* Stephen Labaton, "Hillary Clinton Turned $1,000 into $99,540, White House Says," *New York Times*, March 30, 1994. https://www.nytimes.com/1994/03/30/us/hillary-clinton-turned-1000-into-99540-white-house-says.html

47 *governor of Arkansas in 1978* Labaton, "Hillary Clinton Turned $1,000 into $99,540."

47 *other prepared food items* Thomas Heath, "A Booming Business Runs Afowl of Politics," *Washington Post*, July 23, 1995. https://www.washingtonpost.com/archive/business/1995/07/23/a-booming-business-runs-afowl-of-politics/82c5c420-3c16-4bc2-949a-1975629b52b8/

47 *breast meat for the nugget* Emelyn Rude, "Secrets of the Chicken Nugget: A Surprising History," *Time*, August 2, 2016. https://time.com/4431334/history-chicken-nuggets/

48 *"Mr. Tyson was a father figure for me"* From the interview conducted in 2000 with Buddy Wray that journalist Christopher Leonard shared with me.

48 *"Did you grow up in the church?"* From the interview conducted in 2000 with Buddy Wray that journalist Christopher Leonard shared with me.

48 *"doesn't have to be the smartest"* From the interview conducted

in 2000 with Buddy Wray that journalist Christopher Leonard
shared with me.

48 *smartest person in the room* From the interview conducted in
2000 with Buddy Wray that journalist Christopher Leonard
shared with me.

48 *player in the meatpacking industry* From the interview
conducted in 2000 with Leland Tollett that journalist
Christopher Leonard shared with me.

49 *"can run right over his ass"* From the interview conducted in
2000 with Buddy Wray that journalist Christopher Leonard
shared with me.

49 *the Tyson headquarters in Springdale* Donald Woutat, "Ross
Perot Got It Wrong: In Arkansas, Don Tyson Is the Real Chicken
Man," *Los Angeles Times*, January 10, 1993. https://www
.latimes.com/archives/la-xpm-1993-01-10-fi-1454-story.html

49 *carved over the fireplace* "New Ideas Are Hatched in This
Office," *Wall Street Journal*, December 19, 2001. https://www
.wsj.com/articles/SB1008723961100000000

49 *"nothing wrong with being rich"* From the interview conducted
in 2000 with Leland Tollett that journalist Christopher Leonard
shared with me.

49 *"and growing the company"* From the interview conducted in
2000 with Leland Tollett that journalist Christopher Leonard
shared with me.

49 *"They are two different things"* From the interview conducted
in 2000 with Buddy Wray that journalist Christopher Leonard
shared with me.

50 *interpreters weren't available* From the interview conducted
in 2000 with Buddy Wray that journalist Christopher Leonard
shared with me.

50 *chicken litter in rivers and streams* Keith Schneider, "The 1992
Campaign: Candidate's Record; Arkansas Water Pollution Looms
as a Campaign Issue," *New York Times*, April 21, 1992. https://
www.nytimes.com/1992/04/21/us/1992-campaign-candidate-s
-record-arkansas-water-pollution-looms-campaign-issue.html

50 *pyramids of dried waste* SouthWings, an NGO that provides
volunteer pilots for conservation flights, flew me over
meatpacking facilities in North Carolina.

50 *a sinkhole developed* Schneider, "The 1992 Campaign."
50 *a million gallons a day* Schneider, "The 1992 Campaign."
50 *"an 'imminent health threat emergency'"* Schneider, "The 1992 Campaign."
50 *on environmental issues* Dean Baquet, Jeff Gerth, and Stephen Labaton, "Top Arkansas Lawyer Helped Hillary Clinton Turn Big Profit," *New York Times*, March 18,1994. https://www.nytimes.com/1994/03/18/us/top-arkansas-lawyer-helped-hillary-clinton-turn-big-profit.html
51 *processing plant in the city* Maraniss and Weisskopf, "In Arkansas, the Game Is Chicken."
51 *his candidacy for president* Maraniss and Weisskopf, "In Arkansas, the Game Is Chicken."
51 *budget of Arkansas* Maraniss and Weisskopf, "In Arkansas, the Game Is Chicken."
51 *per election cycle since 2010* Nina Lakhani, "'They rake in the profits—everyone else suffers': US Workers Lose Out as Big Chicken Gets Bigger," *Guardian*, August 11, 2021. https://www.theguardian.com/environment/2021/aug/11/tyson-chicken-indsutry-arkansas-poultry-monopoly
51 *their presidential campaigns* McFadden, "Donald J. Tyson, Food Tycoon."
51 *Chairman and CEO, Don Tyson* "SEC Sues Tyson Foods and Former Chairman Don Tyson for Misleading Disclosure of Perquisites," U.S. Securities and Exchange Commission, April 28, 2005. https://www.sec.gov/news/press/2005-68.htm
51 *and theater tickets* United States District Court for the District of Columbia, Securities Exchange Commission, Plaintiff v. Tyson Foods, Inc. and Donald Tyson. https://www.sec.gov/files/litigation/complaints/comp19208.pdf
51 *and Robert Rauschenberg* Cyd King, "Tyson Art Collection Expands Under Son," Arkansas Online, July 13, 2014. https://www.arkansasonline.com/news/2014/jul/13/tyson-art-collection-expands-under-son-/
52 *"Pennsylvania Avenue in Washington"* Don Tyson, "Tyson Grew Without Clinton," *Oklahoman*, June 2, 1994. https://www.oklahoman.com/story/news/1994/06/02/tyson-grew-without-clinton/62423766007/

52 ***Bill Clinton's first term*** Susan Schmidt, "Tyson Foods Admits Illegal Gifts to Espy," *Washington Post*, December 30, 1997. https://www.washingtonpost.com/archive/politics/1997/12/30 /tyson-foods-admits-illegal-gifts-to-espy/0a09a8fd-8272-4e31 -a542-fb4106180ef3/

52 ***scholarship money for Espy's girlfriend*** Schmidt, "Tyson Foods Admits."

52 ***Tyson Family party in Arkansas*** Schmidt, "Tyson Foods Admits."

53 ***pardoned the Tyson executives*** Schmidt, "Tyson Foods Admits."

53 ***"to do to buy them"*** From the interview conducted in 2000 with Leland Tollett that journalist Christopher Leonard shared with me.

53 ***"which I think is ludicrous to me"*** From the interview conducted in 2000 with Leland Tollett that journalist Christopher Leonard shared with me.

53 ***"That's wrong"*** From the interview conducted in 2000 with Leland Tollett that journalist Christopher Leonard shared with me.

53 ***bad press about food safety issues*** From the interview conducted in 2000 with Leland Tollett that journalist Christopher Leonard shared with me.

53 ***it would take them 165 years*** *Guardian* staff, "John Oliver on the US Meatpacking Industry: 'Things are critical right now,'" *Guardian*, February 22, 2021. https://www.theguardian.com/tv -and-radio/2021/feb/22/john-oliver-meatpacking-industry-last -week-tonight

53 ***hazard that year was $3,700*** *Guardian* staff, "John Oliver on the US Meatpacking Industry."

53 ***at the expense of workers' health*** Alice Driver, "Tyson Says Its Nurses Help Workers. Critics Charge They Stymie OSHA," *Civil Eats*, November 17, 2022. https://civileats.com/2022/11/17 /injured-and-invisible-worker-safety-chicken-hospital-health care-osha-injury/

CHAPTER 4: WHY DOESN'T GOD TAKE ME?

58 ***had only four ambulances*** Mya Frazier, "The Poultry Workers on the Coronavirus Front Line: 'If one of us gets sick, we all get

sick,'" *Guardian*, April 17, 2020. https://www.theguardian.com
/environment/2020/apr/17/chicken-factory-tyson-arkansas-food
-workers-coronavirus

61 *which is often made from ammonia* Casey Tolan and Isabelle
Chapman, "Dangerous Chemical Leaks Have Injured Workers
at One of America's Largest Meat Processors," CNN Business,
May 4, 2023. https://www.cnn.com/2023/05/04/business/tyson
-ammonia-leaks-invs/index.html

61 *meatpacking plants to refrigerate and clean* James Patton, "Gas
in the Great War," KU Medical Center. https://www.kumc
.edu/school-of-medicine/academics/departments/history-and
-philosophy-of-medicine/archives/wwi/essays/medicine/gas-in
-the-great-war.html#:~:text=Chlorine%20was%20deadly%20
against%20unprotected,Chlorine's%20usefulness%20was%20
short%2Dlived

61 *"600 workers were present"* "Chlorine Gas Release Associated
with Employee Language Barrier," Centers for Disease Control
and Prevention, December 7, 2012. https://www.cdc.gov/mmwr
/preview/mmwrhtml/mm6148a1.htm?s_cid=mm6148a1_w

62 *within a few days without issue* Ron Wood, "173 Hospitalized
in Chlorine Gas Leak at Tyson Plant," NWA Online, June 27,
2011. https://www.nwaonline.com/news/2011/jun/27/chlorine
-leak-tyson-plant-hospitalizes-several/#:~:text=June%20
27%2C%202011%20at%209,2011%20at%208%3A09%20p
.m.&text=Springdale%20firefighters%20help%20a%20
woman,about%209%3A15%20am%20Monday

62 *"admitted to intensive-care units"* "Chlorine Gas Release."

62 *one disaster of many recorded* Mya Frazier, "The Poultry
Workers on the Coronavirus Front Line: 'If one of us gets
sick, we all get sick,'" *Guardian*, April 17, 2020. https://www
.theguardian.com/environment/2020/apr/17/chicken-factory
-tyson-arkansas-food-workers-coronavirus

62 *the ones Tyson has acknowledged* Tolan and Chapman,
"Dangerous Chemical Leaks."

63 *facilities to the EPA* Tolan and Chapman, "Dangerous Chemical
Leaks."

63 *reporting to the EPA* Tolan and Chapman, "Dangerous Chemical
Leaks."

63 *of the dangerous chemical* Tolan and Chapman, "Dangerous Chemical Leaks."

63 *that proved fatal* Tolan and Chapman, "Dangerous Chemical Leaks."

63 *some facilities* Tolan and Chapman, "Dangerous Chemical Leaks."

63 *leaving out Arkansas plants* Tolan and Chapman, "Dangerous Chemical Leaks."

63 *down the supply chain* Debbie Berkowitz, Anna D. Goff, Kathleen Marie Fagan, and Monica L. Gerrek, "Do Clinics in Meat and Poultry Plants Endanger Workers?" *AMA Journal of Ethics*, April 2023. https://journalofethics.ama-assn.org /article/do-clinics-meat-and-poultry-plants-endanger -workers/2023-04

65 *needed training to know which chemicals he could mix* Frazier, "The Poultry Workers on the Coronavirus Front Line."

65 *and Tyson's position* City Wire staff, "Tyson Disputes Findings on Chlorine Gas Accident in 2011," *TB&P*, December 7, 2012. https://talkbusiness.net/2012/12/tyson-disputes-findings-on -chlorine-gas-accident-in-2011/

66 *accident was Hispanic* City Wire staff, "Tyson Disputes Findings."

66 *simply made a mistake* City Wire staff, "Tyson Disputes Findings."

66 *caused by individual workers* City Wire staff, "Tyson Disputes Findings."

66 *"we fear losing our jobs"* In a November 18, 2022, email Tyson Foods director of public relations Derek Burleson wrote to me, "Tyson Foods statement: If a team member is injured at work and asks to see a doctor, our nurses are instructed to set up a worker's compensation claim. We pay for worker's compensation approved medical treatment, including consulting with outside doctors, and team members are not required to pay for their own care."

CHAPTER 5: MORE DEAD THAN ALIVE

73 *where she met Magaly Licolli* Olivia Paschal, "For Magaly Licolli, Organizing Poultry Workers Starts with Learning

Together," *Facing South*, June 1, 2021. https://www.facingsouth
.org/2021/06/magaly-licolli-organizing-poultry-workers-starts
-learning-together

77 *benefit the company's bottom line* Michael Grabell, "Tyson
Foods' Secret Recipe for Carving Up Workers' Comp,"
ProPublica, December 11, 2015. https://www.propublica.org
/article/tyson-foods-secret-recipe-for-carving-up-workers
-comp

78 *recommending medical care* Debbie Berkowitz et al., "Do Clinics
in Meat and Poultry Plants Endanger Workers?," *AMA Journal
of Ethics*, April 2023. https://journalofethics.ama-assn.org
/article/do-clinics-meat-and-poultry-plants-endanger-workers
/2023-04

78 *forced to do* Berkowitz et al., "Do Clinics in Meat and Poultry
Plants Endanger Workers?"

80 *"pay for their own care"* Derek Burleson, "Request for comment
on Tyson article for Civil Eats by Oct. 28 at noon" email to Alice
Driver, November 18, 2022.

80 *providing a safe and healthy workplace* Derek Burleson, email
to Alice Driver on November 1, 2022. "The health centers,
which are operated by Marathon Health, provide primary and
preventive care, including health screenings, lifestyle coaching
and health education, as well as behavioral health counseling.
They also collaborate with plant community health providers,
including primary care physicians and specialists, to ensure
appropriate care is delivered." https://www.tysonfoods.com
/news/news-releases/2021/5/tyson-foods-opens-first-pilot-clinic
-promote-culture-health

83 *"ill from work"* In an interview with me Berkowitz said that in
a series of investigations "OSHA also found that in meat and
poultry plants, there are unsupervised first aid staff who often
work outside their legal scope of practice."

83 *they reported injuries* "Better Outreach, Collaboration, and
Information Needed to Help Protect Workers at Meat and
Poultry Plants," United States Government Accountability Office
Report to Congressional Requesters, November 2017. https://
www.gao.gov/assets/gao-18-12.pdf

CHAPTER 6: THE CHAPLAIN

88 *plants in twenty-five states* Frank E. Lockwood, "Tyson's
Chaplains Provide Spiritual Assistance for Workers,"
Arkansas Democrat Gazette, November 5, 2022. https://www
.arkansasonline.com/news/2022/nov/05/tysons-chaplains
-provide-spiritual-assistance-for/#:~:text=Launched%20in%20
2000%2C%20Tyson's%20chaplaincy,red%20states%20
and%20blue%20states

91 *primarily in Florida* Noam Scheiber, "Why Wendy's Is Facing
Campus Protests (It's About the Tomatoes)," *New York Times*,
March 7, 2019. https://www.nytimes.com/2019/03/07/business
/economy/wendys-farm-workers-tomatoes.html

91 *double farmworkers' wages* "Fair Food Program: Frequently
Asked Questions." https://ciw-online.org/ffp_faq/

92 *in the 1980s* Laurie Marshall, "Marshallese in Arkansas: From
the Islands to the Ozarks," May 18, 2021. https://onlyinark.com
/culture/marshallese-in-arkansas-from-the-islands-to-the-ozarks/

92 *Marshall Islands for Arkansas* Olivia Paschal, "The Long Road
to Nuclear Justice for the Marshallese People," *Facing South,*
April 2, 2021. https://www.facingsouth.org/2021/04/long-road
-nuclear-justice-marshallese-people

92 *Free Association in 1986* Suzanne Rust, "How the U.S. Betrayed
the Marshall Islands, Kindling the Next Nuclear Disaster," *Los
Angeles Times*, November 10, 2019. https://www.latimes.com
/projects/marshall-islands-nuclear-testing-sea-level-rise/

93 *or stagnant wages* Debbie Berkowitz et al., "Do Clinics in Meat
and Poultry Plants Endanger Workers?," *AMA Journal of Ethics*,
April 2023. https://journalofethics.ama-assn.org/article/do
-clinics-meat-and-poultry-plants-endanger-workers/2023-04

93 *meatpacking companies like Tyson* Sarah J. Hoffman et
al., "Health of War-Affected Karen Adults 5 Years Post-
Resettlement," *National Library of Medicine*, January 22, 2021.
https://www.ncbi.nlm.nih.gov/pmc/articles/PMC8317216/

93 *Arkansas around 2010* Brenda Bernet, "Refugees Move to
Clarksville," *Northwest Arkansas Democrat Gazette*, June 4,
2012. https://www.nwaonline.com/news/2012/jun/04/refugees
-move-clarksville-20120604/

95 **go to the bathroom** Elizabeth Chuck, "Poultry Workers, Denied Bathroom Breaks, Wear Diapers: Oxfam Report," NBC News, May 12, 2016. https://www.nbcnews.com/business/business -news/poultry-workers-denied-bathroom-breaks-wear-diapers -oxfam-report-n572806

96 **in the US and Canada** Olivia Paschal, "For Magaly Licolli, Organizing Poultry Workers Starts with Learning Together," *The Counter*, June 8, 2021. https://thecounter.org/magaly-licolli -poultry-workers-venceremos-food-chain-workers-alliance /#:~:text=In%202019%20Licolli%20co%2Dfounded,in%20 the%20U.S.%20and%20Canada

CHAPTER 7: THE DISAPPEARANCES

101 **during the pandemic** Alice Driver, "Their Lives on the Line," *New York Review of Books*, April 27, 2021. https://www .nybooks.com/online/2021/04/27/their-lives-on-the-line/

102 **even with fewer workers** "Speed vs. Safety: the Poultry Slaughter Line in the Chicken Industry," *Contratados*, June 26, 2023. https:// contratados.org/en/content/speed-vs-safety-poultry-slaughter -line-chicken-industry#:~:text=In%20some%20cases%2C%20 they%20are,in%20the%20case%20of%20turkeys

102 **175 birds per minute** Rebecca Boehm, "Tyson Spells Trouble for Arkansas: Its Near-Monopoly on Chicken Threatens Farmers, Workers, and Communities," *Union of Concerned Scientists*, August 11, 2021. https://www.ucsusa.org/resources/tyson-spells -trouble#read-online-content

102 **during the pandemic** Leah Douglas, "At Poultry Plants Allowed to Run Faster Processing Lines, a Greater Risk of Covid-19," *Fern's AG Insider*, September 10, 2020. https://thefern.org/ag _insider/at-poultry-plants-allowed-to-run-faster-processing -lines-a-greater-risk-of-covid-19/

102 **spread of the virus** Boehm, "Tyson Spells Trouble."

105 **office work remotely** Dee-Ann Durbin, "Tyson Workers Sue Company over Lack of COVID Protections During Early Days of the Pandemic," *Fortune*, March 7, 2023. https://fortune.com /2023/03/07/tyson-workers-sue-company-over-lack-covid -protections-during-early-days-pandemic/

105 *for the meatpacking industry* Boehm, "Tyson Spells Trouble."

105 *(PPE) and social distancing* "Preventative Actions to Use at All COVID-19 Community Levels," Centers for Disease Control and Prevention. https://www.cdc.gov/coronavirus/2019-ncov/pre vent-getting-sick/prevention.html

106 *cases at meatpacking plants* Olivia Paschal, "Emails Show Tyson's Sway over Arkansas Mayor During COVID Surge in Plants," *Facing South*, February 5, 2021. https://www .facingsouth.org/2021/02/emails-show-tysons-sway-over -arkansas-mayor-during-covid-surge-plants

108 *the end of June* Oliver Laughland and Amanda Holpuch, "'We're modern slaves': How Meat Plant Workers Became the New Frontline in Covid-19 War," *Guardian*, May 2, 2020. https:// www.theguardian.com/world/2020/may/02/meat-plant-workers -us-coronavirus-war

109 *like wearing masks* Paul LeBlanc, "Arkansas GOP Governor Says He Regrets Ban on Mask Mandates as Covid-19 Cases Surge," CNN, August 4, 2021. https://www.cnn.com/2021/08/04 /politics/asa-hutchinson-arkansas-mask-mandate/index.html

109 *do contact tracing* On April 22, 2020, Venceremos announced that it had delivered over 170 signatures from Tyson workers to Tyson management at the Berry Street Plant. The petition demanded that Tyson Foods provide full benefits during the COVID-19 pandemic.

111 *lobbying the Trump administration* Staff report, "How the Trump Administration Helped the Meatpacking Industry Block Pandemic Worker Protections," Select Subcommittee on the Coronavirus Crisis, May 2022. https://www.hsdl.org /?view&did=867324

111 *the* **Arkansas Democrat-Gazette** Zack Budryk, "Tyson Foods Takes Out Full-Page Ad: 'The food supply chain is breaking,'" *The Hill*, April 27, 2020. https://thehill.com/policy/healthcare /494772-tyson-foods-takes-out-full-page-ad-the-food-supply -chain-is-breaking/

112 *keep plants open* Paige Sutherland, Meghna Chakrabarti, and Tim Skoog, "How the Meatpacking Industry Skirted COVID Safety Regulations with the Help of the White House," WBUR, August 11, 2022. https://www.wbur.org/onpoint/2022/08/11

/how-the-meatpacking-industry-chose-profit-over-protecting
-workers

112 *the Defense Production Act of 1950* "Executive Order on
Delegating Authority Under the DPA with Respect to Food Supply
Chain Resources During the National Emergency Caused by the
Outbreak of COVID-19," The White House, April 28, 2020.
https://trumpwhitehouse.archives.gov/presidential-actions
/executive-order-delegating-authority-dpa-respect-food
-supply-chain-resources-national-emergency-caused-outbreak
-covid-19/

112 *related to COVID-19* "Arkansas: State-by-State Covid-19
Guidance." https://www.huschblackwell.com/arkansas-state-by
-state-covid-19-guidance

113 *"the CDC and Tyson"* On March 2, 2021, Gary Mickelson, the
senior director of public relations at Tyson, wrote to me in an
email, "Our policy is that team members should not come to
work if they have COVID-19 or have been exposed to someone
who has the virus but rather should stay home and focus on
getting better—and we continue to communicate this regularly to
all team members. Team members who test positive are eligible
to receive short-term disability pay and may return to work only
when they have met the criteria established by both the CDC and
Tyson."

114 *test positive for COVID-19* Tim Fitzsimons, "Suit Alleges Tyson
Foods Plant Manager Bet on How Many Workers Would Get
Coronavirus," NBC News, November 19, 2020. https://www
.nbcnews.com/news/us-news/suit-alleges-tyson-food-plant
-manager-bet-how-many-workers-n1248230

114 *"don't go hungry"* Laurel Wamsley, "Tyson Foods Fires 7 Plant
Managers over Betting Ring on Workers Getting COVID-19,"
NPR, December 16, 2020. https://www.npr.org/sections
/coronavirus-live-updates/2020/12/16/947275866/tyson-foods
-fires-7-plant-managers-over-betting-ring-on-workers-getting
-covid-19

114 *as early as March* Fitzsimons, "Suit Alleges."

114 *"based on the findings"* Wamsley, "Tyson Foods Fires 7 Plant
Managers."

115 *"exporting chicken to China"* Talk Business & Politics,

"Coronavirus Slowing Tyson Exports to China," ABC 7, February 20, 2020. https://katv.com/news/local/coronavirus-slowing-tyson -exports-to-china

115 *severe cases of COVID* Joshua Keating, "Why a Pacific Islander Community in Arkansas Became a COVID Hot Spot," *Slate*, September 15, 2020. https://slate.com/technology/2020/09 /marshallese-covid-arkansas.html

115 *"deaths in the region"* "Arkansas Atoll," apple.com. https:// podcasts.apple.com/us/podcast/arkansas-atoll/id1544326587

117 *half of whom were Marshallese* "Arkansas Atoll." https:// podcasts.apple.com/us/podcast/arkansas-atoll/id1544326587

117 *19 percent of the COVID cases* "Arkansas Atoll." https:// podcasts.apple.com/us/podcast/arkansas-atoll/id1544326587

121 *COVID-related protections and pay* Olivia Paschal and Roland Zenteno, "Workers Say Arkansas' Poultry Giants Aren't Protecting Them from COVID-19," *Facing South*, April 28, 2020.

CHAPTER 8: ABSENCE IS A SILENT PAIN

125 *Secretary of Agriculture Sonny Perdue* Madison McVan, Eli Hoff, and Sky Chadde, "Trump Ag Secretary Sonny Perdue Personally Lobbied to Keep Meatpacking Plants Open During Pandemic, Emails Show," *Investigate Midwest*, July 2, 2021. https://investigatemidwest.org/2021/07/02/trump-ag-secretary -sonny-perdue-personally-lobbied-to-keep-meatpacking-plants -open-during-pandemic-emails-show/

125 *absenteeism was not acceptable* Staff report, "How the Trump Administration Helped the Meatpacking Industry Block Pandemic Worker Protections," Select Subcommittee on the Coronavirus Crisis, May 2022. https://www.hsdl.org/?view&did=867324

126 *"instead of coming to work"* Staff report, "How the Trump Administration."

126 *470,000 meatpacking workers* Stephen Groves and Sophia Tareen, "U.S. Meatpacking Industry Relies on Immigrant Workers. But a Labor Shortage Looms," *Los Angeles Times*, May 26, 2020. https://www.latimes.com/food/story/2020-05-26 /meatpacking-industry-immigrant-undocumented-workers

126 *involved non-White workers* David Pitt, "CDC: Minorities Affected Much More in Meatpacking Outbreaks," AP, July 8, 2020. https://apnews.com/article/12c6f7dd8888b7f2a174ae4ba8f06b67

126 *tested positive for the virus* Nathan Owens, "At Tyson, 13% of Workers Infected," *Arkansas Democrat Gazette*, June 20, 2020. https://www.arkansasonline.com/news/2020/jun/20/at-tyson-13-of-workers-infected/

126 *"in terms of our nation's meat supply"* Parija Kavilanz and Danielle Wiener-Bronner, "Coronavirus Committee: Meat Companies Lied About Impending Shortage and Put Workers At Risk," CNN Business, May 13, 2022. https://www.cnn.com/2022/05/12/business/meat-companies-investigation-covid-response/index.html

127 *"with COVID-positive tests"* Staff report, "How the Trump Administration."

128 *"the VP's office are not able to stop it"* Staff report, "How the Trump Administration."

128 *"their operations and normal work schedules"* Staff report, "How the Trump Administration."

129 *resulting in the death of at least 176* Staff report, "How the Trump Administration."

140 *bipartisan failure to protect meatpacking workers* Dave Dickey, "Opinion: Big Meat Lobbyists Are Bullying Lawmakers into Submission," *Investigate Midwest*, June 1, 2023. https://investigatemidwest.org/2023/06/01/big-meat-lobbyists-are-bullying-lawmakers-into-submission/

141 *"exporting meat to China"* Michael Corkery and David Yaffe-Bellany, "As Meat Plants Stayed Open to Feed Americans, Exports to China Surged," *New York Times*, June 16, 2020. https://www.nytimes.com/2020/06/16/business/meat-industry-china-pork.html

CHAPTER 9: THE ARMADILLOS

164 *GoFundMe page to raise money to support her* Ana Tapia, "Mother of 2 and Expecting Severely Burned," GoFundMe, May 10, 2022. https://www.gofundme.com/f/gloria-and-her-children

CHAPTER 10: THE LAWSUIT

171 *269 worker deaths in the first year of the pandemic* Staff report, "How the Trump Administration Helped the Meatpacking Industry Block Pandemic Worker Protections," Select Subcommittee on the Coronavirus Crisis, May 2022. https://www.hsdl.org/?view&did=867324

179 *greenhouse workers often have few protections* John Bowe, "The Immokalee Way: Protecting Farmworkers Amid a Pandemic," *Nation*, September 14, 2020. https://www.thenation.com/article/society/farming-labor-contractors-coronavirus/

184 *from Black and immigrant communities* Rachel Aviv, "Punishment by Pandemic," *New Yorker*, June 15, 2020. https://www.newyorker.com/magazine/2020/06/22/punishment-by-pandemic

185 *"to call 'brother' or lose their jobs"* Jane Mayer, "Tycoons Exploit the Pandemic," *New Yorker*, July 13, 2020. https://www.newyorker.com/magazine/2020/07/20/how-trump-is-helping-tycoons-exploit-the-pandemic

185 *turnover in any given year* Eyal Press, *Dirty Work: Essential Jobs and the Hidden Toll of Inequality in America* (Farrar, Straus and Giroux, 2021), 166–67.

CONCLUSION: ROBOTS AND LAB-GROWN MEAT

201 *"no longer have to have Hispanics"* From the interviews conducted in 2000 with Leland Tollett and Buddy Wray that journalist Christopher Leonard shared with me.

203 *"between humans and nonhuman animals"* Alicia Kennedy, *No Meat Required* (Beacon Press, 2003), 11.

204 *for planting and harvesting* Ligaya Mishan, "In a Starving World, Is Eating Well Unethical?" *New York Times Style Magazine*, March 18, 2022. https://www.nytimes.com/2022/03/18/t-magazine/indulgence-starvation-food-inequality.html#:~:text=EATING%20IS%20INTRINSICALLY%20selfish.,the%20American%20bioethicist%20Leon%20R

204 *"no sacrifice required"* Mishan, "In a Starving World."

205 *"yet capital is leading us right back"* Kennedy, *No Meat Required*, 148.

206 *slaughtered cows to create lab-grown meat* Tom Philpott, "The Bloody Secret Behind Lab-Grown Meat," *Mother Jones*, April 2022. https://www.motherjones.com/environment/2022/03/lab-meat-fetal-bovine-serum-blood-slaughter-cultured/

INDEX

ABOUT THE AUTHOR

Alice Driver is a James Beard Award–winning writer from the Ozark Mountains in Arkansas. Driver is the author of *More or Less Dead* (University of Arizona Press, 2015). Driver is the translator of *Abecedario de Juárez* (University of Texas Press, 2022). This is her first trade book.